ODE OF THE TRAVELER

ODE OF THE TRAVELER

The Journey in Verse

Jim Menge

With Illustrations by Derick Lowe

Sierra Pine
Productions

Ode of the Traveler: The Journey in Verse
Copyright © 2025 by Jim Menge
All rights reserved.

Printed in the United States of America

ISBN: 979-89925441-2-1 (Hardcover)
ISBN: 00-0-0000000-0-0 (eBook)
Library of Congress Control Number: 0000000000

An Imprint of Sierra Pine Productions
9800 Harpers Lane, Suite 5066
Dallas, TX 75019 USA

For speaking engagements, bulk orders, or inquiries, visit:
https://JimMenge.com

CONTENTS

image (c) by Mackenzie Christy
My always traveling; this Scottish cloak & handsome hat.
Photographed by our skylight moonlight 2016
Post stage III ovarian cancer;

vi

WALLOW OR WALK?

Discovery
Deciding
Remembering
Recovery
I only travel; if the hat & cape go
My journey always intentionally; "rough".
Here she lives until the next treks are in-
bound.
For tired are the threads I've sewn....
And weary the seamstress that weaves the life
I live.
Wool
Layers of love
Thick she is.
It's an artistic cathartic walk.....
Booking miles of isles & tears of growth.
Sitting deciding about life....
Wallow or walk?
- Me

Mackenzie Christy

Also by Jim Menge

Bushido Business
Never Travel in a Straight Line

To my friend,

Kyle Lowe,
1961 – 2024

whose journey shaped so many others ~
and continues quietly through these pages.

~

ACKNOWLEDGEMENTS

This is a book long in the making. Some walked beside me. Some waited patiently at the gate. Many handed me their stories, trusting I'd carry them well. I am grateful to each.

Nicole Morgan who encouraged me to stretch my voice beyond comfort into something new. Your insight helped me write toward places inward I hadn't yet seen, and your belief in my work offered more light than you know.

Lena Koury who as an early reader regularly sent me questions that stretched me, comments that made me smile, and epistles of examples. I could fit her invaluable musings into a suitcase of love that I would have to check under the plane.

John Halcomb who unearthed a poetic piece I wrote years ago and gently turned it into "*I'm a Traveling Man*". Thank you for seeing past the scribbles, helping me expand my vision, and letting me wax poetic about Heathrow Airport ~ a tired traveler's resting place that somehow always felt like home.

Dave Baird who showered advice on how to travel with a loving spouse and ideal kids with grace and humor. Thank you for Havana, Prague, and taking the train with me to Berlin.

Pam Leigh, thank you for reading early drafts with a clear mind and a curious heart. Your questions sharpened my writing. Your encouragement lightened it. And for creating a clear path walking forward toward what mattered.

Mackenzie Christy whose photos and ode gave this book its emotional compass, "*Wallow or Walk?*". I'm grateful to be walking ~ and occasionally wallowing ~ alongside you.

Brad Bennett who, since the late 1900's, has been closer than a friend. Thank you, Brad for Seville, Tarifa, Gibraltar, and my endless writing and life musings. The years are good to us.

Thank you, Joey and Tricia Fox. Your travels strengthen
the love between you; your writings in this book and warm
encouragement strengthen me. I love you both.

Demetrius, my son and fellow traveler ~ thank you for teaching
me, laughing and reminding me that every journey is better
when shared: Amman, Majuro, Lhasa, New Caledonia, Cannes.

Johanna, my daughter and quiet compass. Your loving sarcastic
wisdom and one raised eyebrow during our one-day trips were
magic for me. Your love is precious. Thank you.

My mother and father who each influenced my love for the
globe, for lessons on the similarities and differences in people.

To my colleagues at Sabre dealing with me over the years, to
the people and places I mention throughout this book. You
made me realize that the traveler is more than the travel, more
than the journey, more than the pain. Thank you.

Derick Lowe, son of Kyle... your encouragement, inspiration
and time are all anyone in my spot could ask. Trust, truth and
tenderness are what you are all about.

In the midst of your own grief, you offered your creativity with
grace. What you brought to this book isn't just artwork ~ it is
presence. Through each sketch, I hear your father's voice, feel
your heart, and know the quiet strength that runs through
both of you.

You don't just illustrate the odes ~ you deepen them. You
turn moments into memory, and memory into meaning. Your
fingerprints are on every page, and for that, I'm endlessly
grateful.

Thank you from my heart.

A SPECIAL ACKNOWLEDGEMENT

This book is dedicated to my friend, Kyle Lowe ‑ a fellow traveler, straight shooter, and soul whose presence still lingers in me.

I met Kyle in 2013, when I'd just stepped into an unfamiliar industry. While others welcomed me with platitudes or polite silence, Kyle offered strong clarity. With a grin and a dose of honesty, he looked me in the eye and said,

"Jim, you have no idea what you are getting yourself into. Just don't screw it up."

That was Kyle: no frills, no filter, always to the point.

He reminded me that people mattered more than platforms, and that despite our work, we were still allowed to laugh. I took flights; Kyle took stock of people. His knowledge of the world was encyclopedic, his humor bone-dry. He'd rope me into tech repairs or gym trips and then tell me what I got wrong.

At conferences, he was part Muppet critic, part one-liner machine. "Here comes the geek parade," he'd mutter. Or, "That speech? Bird droppings." He never missed.

The last time I saw Kyle was at the Las Vegas airport for the redeye back to DFW. He looked calm. Lighter. I told him about this book ‑ true to form, he gave me his usual sign-off:

"Jim, just don't screw it up."

> I miss Kyle.
> I listen for Kyle at the airport, in the gym, at a restaurant.
> I just hope I didn't screw it up too badly.

A Journey Shared

By Derick Lowe

Change has been the cornerstone of my life's journey.

Born in Taiwan and raised across multiple countries and six different U.S. states, I've always known the ebb and flow of new experiences. My father's work was the catalyst for our nomadic lifestyle, but it was he and my mother's encouragement to embrace diversity that truly shaped my worldview. We were never confined to a single perspective or belief system. Instead, we were taught to be culturally curious, making each move an adventure to look forward to.

That adaptability served me well when I met Jim in London in 2014. I was finishing university and found myself with an unexpected opportunity: a chance to pitch an idea to the president of a travel company – Jim himself. Our shared passion for travel and people forged an immediate connection, leading to an internship that grew into a lasting professional and personal relationship.

Travel, much like change, has been a constant thread woven through my life. It's a passion I inherited from my father, whose work took us around the world and whose spirit of adventure never waned. I still remember a conversation with him in 2022, when I expressed my desire to work with him and Jim on a future business venture. His response: "Jim is a good guy – we'll work together one day." Now, those words feel prophetic.

The greatest change I've had to face came with my father's passing in early 2024. The loss left an aching void – but it also opened unexpected doors for growth and connection. Jim's continued presence during that time was a comfort. Our weekly coffee meetings became a safe space to share stories, to laugh, and at times, to grieve.

When Jim asked if I would illustrate some of his odes, I hesitated. It had been years since I'd picked up that part of myself. But in accepting his offer, I found a way to honor my father's memory ~ and to rediscover something long buried. Each illustration became a journey in itself, a way to travel through emotions and memories.

This book, and my contribution to it, represents the intersection of so many threads from my life. It's a testament to the power of change, the enduring influence of my father, and the transformative magic of travel. Through these pages, I've reconnected with creativity, with meaning ~ and with him.

As you read Jim's stories and see the illustrations that accompany them, I hope you'll be inspired to embrace your own journey of change. Even in loss, there are new paths waiting. And sometimes, they lead us not away from love ~ but back to it.

~

Preface

"What does this journey awaken in me?"

This is the question this book asks you, the reader, to consider.

This collection began as a whisper, scribbled on napkins in Istanbul cafés, on a ferry deck crossing the Baltic, the dark Atlantic waters, between departure boards at London Heathrow Airport that promised everywhere and arrival gates that delivered transformation. Some pieces emerged from Hong Kong jet lag at 3 AM. Others from the quiet awe of watching sunrise over a Paris rooftop or hearing my name called across a crowded airport by someone I didn't expect to see.

What unfolded was not a record of where I've been, but a deeper inquiry: Why do we go? What calls us forward? And who do we become when we surrender to the road?

Travel doesn't begin at the boarding gate. It starts with a feeling ~ a quiet longing, a sudden calling, an ache that says elsewhere. Over four decades of wandering through more than 100 countries, I've come to understand that every journey is driven by something invisible: hope, hunger, the whisper of possibility that guides us toward places we didn't know we needed to find.

I've traveled out of necessity ~ work that demanded movement. For celebration ~ milestones in foreign cities. For connection ~ following love, friendship, and kindred spirits. And for transcendence ~ those pilgrimages of my soul that stripped everything away except what mattered most.

But more than anything, I traveled to listen. To the rhythm of unfamiliar languages. To strangers who became teachers. To the quieter voice within that only speaks when we're far from everything we think we know.

The format mirrors travel itself ‑ unpredictable seatmates, intimate moments, alive with sudden turns. These are not Instagram captions or travel tips. They are emotional waypoints, each tied to a moment that shifted something inside me, each ode is a footprint ‑ small, specific, sincere.

Why "ode"? Because these are not just poems ‑ they are offerings. Tributes to moments that mattered. This sunrise. This stranger's kindness. This breaking point that became a breakthrough. Odes carry reverence. They say, "the world showed me something sacred, and I want to honor it."

Authenticity anchors everything here. These words are raw and true, capturing not the postcard version of travel but the real texture ‑ the blisters in Spain, breakthroughs in New York, the missed connections in Chicago that led to unexpected grace, the way distance can teach us about closeness.

As St. Jerome wrote, powerful writing is "not so much words, as thunderings." Percy Shelley reminded us that "poetry lifts the veil from the hidden beauty of the world." In that spirit, I invite you to lift the veil on your own journey ‑ the one you've taken, the one you're planning, and the one that may be calling to you right now.

Ode of the Traveler is not instruction ‑ it's invitation. Not itinerary ‑ it's inner archaeology. Let it be mirror, map, and compass as you discover what the journey awakens in you.

Enjoy the chaos. Embrace the journey.

INTRODUCTION

A Journey Beyond Movement

At seven years old, I sat cross-legged on the floor in our indoor patio, turning the heavy pages of my father's Coast Guard photo album. The cover was a welded mosaic of foreign coins ~ New Guinea pence and shillings, Australian pennies, Balboa coins, Philippine pesos, and currencies I couldn't pronounce each one a doorway to somewhere else. Inside, black and white photographs were fastened to black pages with white corner tabs, places that looked nothing like our Florida town.

I didn't know then that I was already traveling ~ that each turned page was teaching my heart a language it would spend a lifetime learning to speak.

By thirteen, I claimed Miami International Airport as my second home. While other kids spent weekends at the mall, I haunted the departure gates, watching Convairs and Constellations arrive from places I could only find in atlases. Pan Am, Eastern, National Airlines ~ carriers that ruled the skies in South Florida, the Caribbean, Latin & South America. Every take off left whispers that asked the same question, "What if you followed me?"

At fifteen, I took my first flight ~ in a Cessna with an instructor who didn't ask too many questions, parents unaware. At sixteen, my first commercial flight, parents still unaware. At eighteen, the Air Force stationed me in Japan, where I learned that distance isn't measured in miles but in moments. Hopping military flights to Iwo Jima, Hawaii, Seoul the Philippines ~ each destination reshaping what I thought I knew about the world ~ and myself.

Somewhere between working for American Airlines after the Air Force, giving speeches about technology that linked distant places, and having a business card that read "Evangelist," I realized something shifted. I wasn't just moving through the world anymore. The world was moving through me.

At Virtuoso, the premier luxury travel network, I learned the language of *transformational*, *affluent*, and *once-in-a-lifetime experiences*.

Every journey – even the delayed flights and wrong turns – carries the possibility of transformation. The question isn't whether the experience will be extraordinary. The question is whether we're awake enough to receive it.

The Traveler's Journey

Travel is poetry in motion – a rhythm of longing, discovery, and return. But the true destination is never a place; it's who we become along the way.

Some land on comfort and convenience – **tourists** collecting snapshots of what's already been seen. They choose guided experiences, well-reviewed restaurants, and structured itineraries that offer discovery within a framework of security.

Some evolve into **travelers** – embracing uncertainty, collecting experiences instead of just photos. They venture beyond tour groups, eat where locals eat, sleep where guidebooks fear to tread. The unknown becomes friend rather than foe. Many **influencers** live here, turning experience into audience.

A dedicated few become travel **experts** – masters of logistics who know which train to catch, which customs officer to approach, which smile opens doors. They speak the language of miles and points, visas and connections.

But expertise is still about the external world. The travel **sage** transcends mechanics to mine meaning. They understand that missed flights teach patience, that getting lost reveals resilience, that every goodbye carries the seed of transformation. For sages, travel becomes a teacher that shapes how they see everything ~ not just destinations, but daily life.

And then ~ if the journey lasts long enough, if the heart stays open enough ~ something profound emerges. The travel **mystic** stops traveling to places and begins traveling through consciousness itself. Movement becomes meditation. Geography becomes geology of the soul. They discover that every journey was always an inner journey, every step a conversation with the divine.

I've walked the Camino de Santiago until my body broke and my spirit rebuilt itself. In the silence of the Atacama Desert, absence of sound became a presence all its own. Three days by train to Lhasa, watching the world rise toward heaven, something inside me learned to breathe at altitude. In the sacred halls of London's Daunt Books and Strouds, I understood that books are portals and bookstores are temples.

Now I write about these deeper places, speak about travel as spiritual practice, guide others toward their own inner pilgrimages. I find myself somewhere between sage and mystic, still learning what it means when the road becomes not just a path through the world, but a path through the self.

Most stop here. A rare few go further.

The travel illuminary no longer travels to discover or escape.

The road is simply the way they breathe. The world is their temple, every encounter a prayer, every step an offering. They've dissolved the boundary between journey and destination, between traveler and path. They become living invitations for others to begin their own awakening..

Beyond This Journey

Ode of the Traveler is an invitation: to move through the world with presence and intention ‐ so the journey unfolds not just around you, but within you. The unexpected detour might be the destination. The magic will find you in places you didn't expect to go.

Perhaps you're somewhere on this path. Perhaps you're just approaching the threshold. This book doesn't tell you how to travel. It invites you to travel differently.

To listen. To see. To **let the journey shape you.**

The Book

What you hold in your hands began as whispers ‐ fragments caught between departure and arrival, scribbled in margins and captured in the spaces between heartbeats. These odes carry three kinds of wisdom: the deep knowing that comes from years of wandering (♦), the emotional truth of connection and loss (♥), and the necessary humor that softens the craziness of the journey (☻).

You're about to join a path to somewhere you've only imagined. We have no idea what waits ahead ‐ the way morning light will fall differently on unfamiliar walls, how bread tastes when baked with flour you've never tasted, how your legs will feel after walking cobblestones worn smooth by centuries of other footsteps. The way jet lag will scramble your sense of time until you exist in a floating present. How a stranger's kindness will catch you off guard, or how climbing that hill will leave you breathless in ways you didn't expect.

The unexpected detour might be the destination. The magic will find you in places you didn't plan to go. And if you feel the road whispering something deeper – something that goes beyond movement into meaning – then you're ready for what lies ahead.

Perhaps you'll find yourself moving through these stages: from tourist to traveler to expert to sage. And maybe, if you listen closely enough, the mystic path will call to you, too.

This is your boarding call.

The journey has begun.

♦

☺

♥

SECTION 1

WHO LONGS TO GO?

AWAKENING THE TRAVELER WITHIN

Don't go back to sleep.
The breeze at dawn has secrets to tell you.
Don't go back to sleep.

~ Rumi

In the stillness of the night, the dreamer's heart takes flight. Desires unfold with each star a place whispering, "**Come find me.**"

Dreaming is where it all begins ~ a canvas for the mind. It's the screen on which the story of our inner self plays out, where **yearning** becomes the **spark** of every journey. Not a step, but a feeling, a pull toward the unknown.

Do we choose the dream, or does the dream choose us? That's the question I return to time and again. I've seen it in others, too ~ those far-off glances when they speak of a place they've never been yet somehow know is meant for them.

When the dreamer awakens, **the world has shifted**. A new thought, a new place, a new adventure rises to meet them.

Like Rumi's Guesthouse,
we welcome each possibility,
each longing,
knowing they are part of what makes us alive.

3

Whispers of the World ◆
Miami International Airport

At 13,
    I watched Convairs, Constellations, and Concorde
    Douglas, Lockheed and Martin's land ~
    arriving from places I only knew from maps,
    names unpronounced in school and daydreams.

Every departure gate held secrets,
    every arrival board whispered possibilities:
    London, Lima, New York, Martinique ~
    places that lived only in my imagination.

Carriers that ruled the day,
    Pan Am, Eastern and National Airlines,
    Braniff in all it's colors,
    Varig and Viasa; LAB and Equiatoriana
    Whispers now gone.

The roar of props and jet engines spoke a language
    I was desperate to understand.
Each jet trail leaving promises across the sky,
    carrying stories I longed to make my own.

The world spoke softly to me,
    each whisper pulling me closer,
    etching its call into my heart
    until the whispers became a song
    I couldn't help but follow.

The world whispered, and I listened.

The Travel Seed ♦
My Friend Brad

"Travel

    lays the seeds

        that become

           the future you."

The Edge of Discovery ♦

I stand on the edge of **wanderlust**,
    where maps promise stories untold.
Every place I have not been
    pulls at me.

There are cities that call to me,
    their voices heard from early on.
There are paths that lead to nowhere -
    or perhaps everywhere,
    maybe even anywhere.

The pull is endless,
    not a need to escape (*Atacama*),
    but a need to **belong to something larger**:
    the **clamor of markets** (*Istanbul*),
    the **hush of ancient ruins** (*Rhodes*),
    the **laugh of a stranger becoming a friend** (*Dubai*).

Wanderlust is not a place;
    it's a fleeting, weightless moment,
    where possibility stretches ahead.

I chart no course,
    for I don't need a destination -
    just the **promise**
    of what I might find,
    and what might find me.

Tracing Choices ♥
Driving Through the Ozarks

The road through the hills unspools and winds.
    Maps don't capture the **detours**,
    the way we **pause**,
    the way we **shift**.

Your finger traces the route.
We stop at the crossroads -
    not lost, but not certain.
You point this way.

Some choices are easy -
    a left turn here, a right turn there.
But others, like us,
    are meant to be discovered **as we go**.

We take the road that curves,
    where signs are absent, where the path is unknown.
Somewhere between the **leaving** and the **arriving**,
    we make a place of our own.

The sun gets lower and the shadows stretch.
    If we lose the path, we'll make a new one.
    If we lose each other, **we'll find our way back**.

We're committed to the journey -
    to the paths we've yet to find,
    to the way we **map each other**,
    to the road that always leads us home.

And,
    to the journey of us.

Gravity Between Us ♥
When You Realize Someone Shares Your Wanderlust

I didn't know
    I could want a person the same way
    I've always wanted the world.

Not to possess ~
    but to walk beside.

To hear your breath catch
    when the Duomo appears magically before you.
To laugh with you
    when we almost miss the train to Portland
    and find a better story instead.
To plot a new path
    when we almost lose the last seat
    from Albuquerque.

There is a kind of gravity
    between people who are
    drawn to elsewhere.

Not just travelers.
    Seekers, feelers.
    Those who leave space in their suitcase
    for the unexpected.

We don't need control,
    we just need wonder.

This is our compass:
    Not where we're going,
        but how we move ~
    together.

The Compass of the World ♦
For my friend, Paul

London, where history and dreams converge,
 the city at 0° ~
 a place to center,
 to mark beginnings
 and measure journeys.

I walk its streets,
 where whispers of the world meet the present.
 At Stanfords and Daunt,
  maps unfold,
  guiding me to lands I've only dreamed of.

From here, the world radiates:
 North, to the highlands and castles of Scotland.
 East, to Istanbul and the trade winds of story.
 West, to the Atlantic and the promise of the New World.
 South, to Greenwich,
  where space and time intertwine

I linger at corners that feel familiar,
 though I've never been there before.
 A voice calls from a narrow alley ~
  not mine, but meant for me.
 The city doesn't ask for permission
  to enter your heart.
  It already has.

The Thames flows steady, timeless,
 a ribbon of history threading the past to now.
Big Ben chimes, marking not just time,
 but the **moments I carry forward**.

In this city,
 I feel the **pull of every place I've been**
 and **the call of every destination waiting ahead**.

London breathes,
 alive with the rhythm of its past and present.
 A city of poets, lovers, and explorers.

London, the city of dreams, **holds me**.
 Not just a place to visit,
  but a place to belong –
  where every journey begins again.

Following the Whisper ♦

I see the streak of a plane over a mountain,
    in the early evening,
    as the sun sets.

Who sits within the plane?
Dreamers, pilgrims, backpackers, strangers.
    Their stories touching mine
        through miles of shared space.

The plane appears, then fades,
    like the boy I once was,
    watching them from below,
    dreaming of distant places.

The planes, the names, the places, the people -
    many have disappeared or changed,
    but the **whisper to move**, to leave,
        to return grows louder, becoming
        the **sound of a jet engine**,
        the **airport announcements**,
        the **wave against the ship**, and
        the **train conductors voice**.

Now I fly beyond those dreams,
    no longer chasing whispers -
    but dancing with them,
    step by measured step,
    across the waiting sky.

The Dreamer's Voyage ♦
Queen Mary 2: New York - Southampton

The ultimate escape,
    far from shore, aboard an oceanliner
    suspended between
        the sea floor and the sky,
    each surge revealing the ocean's might.

Each day, we sail toward a new sunrise,
    the deep ocean's rhythm,
    the early morning light,
    the oncoming evening sunset,
    the dark night stars,
    the gently rocking sleep,
    the dreams of voyages.

The sea holds space
    for those who need no map -
    only a direction
    and time to drift into becoming.

The world is mine to sail.

The Wave and the Swell ♦

For Captain Aseem Hashmi, Master of the Queen Mary 2

In the vast expanse of the ocean,
    a wave surfaces,
    playful, transient,
    shaped by the whims of the wind.

Beneath, **a swell rises**,
    deep, powerful,
    born of distant storms,
    carrying the memory of far away places.

The wave is the moment's whisper;
    the swell,
    the ocean's enduring voice.

The traveler learns to listen to both –
    to chase the wave's thrill
    while honoring the swell's truth.

Desert Stars ♦
My friends, Mohammed & David

Dubai, where the old world meets the new,
    desert sands whisper ancient tales,
    while glass towers pierce the sky,
    reflecting a city of tomorrow.

The dunes shift with the wind, timeless,
    as the city pulses relentlessly.
    A caravan across these sands is now
        a highway of paved with fulfilled ambition.

Lights dancing across the skyline,
    the desert holds its silence,
    a reminder of what came before.

Here, vision races toward excellence,
    where every challenge becomes foundation
    for towers that dare to touch
    the edge of human possibility.

Beneath the stars, both worlds collide ‑
    one, eternal and still;
    the other, restless and rising.

In this place,
    every step is a bridge
    between **what was**,
        and **what is becoming**.

Navigating Us ♥

Traveling together sounds effortless
    until the road curves in two directions at once..
Your map points north,
    mine points toward an adventure
    neither of us planned.

You rise with the sun,
    I sleep past the first train.
You crave schedules,
    I wander like the breeze,
        trusting curiosity over itineraries.

The miles stretch us
    into laughter over wrong turns,
    into quiet, shared sunsets,
    into the art of **navigating each other,**
        one detour at a time.

We lose track of time,
    but find ourselves
    in the rhythm of the road,
    where together always feels
    like the right destination.

You watched to learn my wanderings,
    quietly gathering clues.
You felt what I never said.
    a language between steps.

You longed to unfold next to me.

Becoming the Whisper ◆

Once, I chased whispers across continents,
 following dreams that pulled me forward
 into places I could only imagine.

Then, I walked beside those whispers,
 learning their language,
 becoming part of their story.

Now, I find myself changing -
 a quiet voice in another's dream,
 a gentle guide that awakens wanderlust
  in those who stand where I once stood,
  watching planes fly possibilities across the sky.

The journey continues:
 from **dreamer to guide**,
 from **seeker to mentor**,
 from **listener to voice**.

Each step I took has led me here -
 to this moment of transformation,
 where experience becomes wisdom,
 and wisdom becomes **inspiration**.

Now, I dream for others -
 each journey becoming part
 of the **endless story of the traveler**
 that calls to wandering hearts.

When Paths Are Chosen ♦
An ode to the unseen companions of every step

The road ahead is mine to walk,
    yet I am never truly alone.

Beneath my feet,
    the earth remembers
    those who came before,
        their footsteps pressed into time.

Their voices are the wind at my back,
    the quiet knowing in my bones.
    Not demanding.
    Not commanding.
        Waiting to see which way I go.
    Seeing their path, I
        forage my own way.

Choice is not a burden,
    but an inheritance.

A gift from those who stood at crossroads,
    who wandered,
    who wondered,
    who dared to walk forward.

In the spaces between my steps,
    a presence moves ~
        not memory, but something alive,
        breathing with the rhythm of the next.
    The unseen companion whispers
        when the path disappears,
        and steadies my hand
        when I reach for door.

I cannot yet see. And so I step,
    knowing **I do not walk alone.**

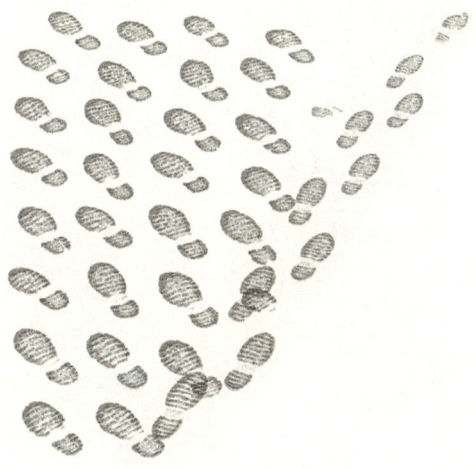

THE CALL BEFORE THE JOURNEY

Forget safety.
Live where you fear to live.
Destroy your reputation.
Be notorious.

~ Rumi

Every journey begins in stillness ~ when an image, a name, or a half-formed thought settles into the mind and refuses to leave.

A **longing without a destination**.
A pull toward something unnamed.

What calls us forward?

Is it the hunger for something new, or the quiet knowing of a soul that recognizes its next horizon? We dream of places we've never seen yet somehow know we're meant to find.

- What draws us to certain places before we've set foot in them?
- Do we chase the unknown, or are we answering an echo?
- Is the dream itself pointing us toward who we're becoming?

Perhaps what awaits
is not just a place,
but a **version of ourselves**
we have yet to meet ~
one that has been waiting
for us all along.

SECTION 2

WHAT IS WAITING TO BE FOUND?

DECISIONS THAT SHAPE DESTINATIONS

*"The future stands still,
but we move in infinite space."*

– Rainer Maria Rilke, Letters to a Young Poet

Dreaming sets the stage, and **discovering stirs the soul** ~ but, deciding is where the journey begins to take form. It's the leap, the moment when you take the plunge from *possibility* to plan.

Deciding is when the dream shifts from someday to now.

I've felt it ~ that spark of clarity when I stop imagining and start **committing**. Deciding isn't just picking dates or clicking *"book now."*

Deciding is a vow to myself that **this dream, this journey, will happen**.

For you, the decision phase may feel like a ritual. Dates take on meaning, reservations become promises, and maps morph into guides for what's to come.

This is the point of no return,
    where ideas turn into actions,
    and the dreams awaken us.

It's **exhilarating** and **terrifying** all at once, isn't it? But that's the beauty of it.

The future isn't just a dream anymore ~
    it's a destination
        waiting for you.

27

A Pilgrim on the Road to Everywhere ♦

It started early.
    A longing, a pull, a whisper of elsewhere.
    I wasn't running away ~ I was reaching toward.
    Distant places felt closer than the ones I knew,
        as if my soul had already left footprints
            in lands I had yet to see.

Even when the world sent me somewhere,
    I took my own path.

    Athens wasn't enough ~ I *sought* Dushanbe.
    Kuala Lumpur? Close ~ but I *needed* Rangoon.
    Florence ~ the *gateway* to San Marino.
    Trieste ~ the *portal* to Slovenia
    Nice, *fabulous.*
    Monaco, *famous.*

Every trip was a map with edges left unfinished,
        an invitation
        ...not just to go ~
        but to go further.

Someone once wrote, *Jim is a Pilgrim on the Road to Everywhere.*
    Maybe they were right.
    Maybe I have never been content with **arrival** ~
        only the possibility of what lies **beyond**.

With intention and reverence,
    every journey can become sacred.

"With a deepening of focus, keen preparation,
attention to the path below our feet, and
respect for the destination at hand, it is possible
to transform even the most ordinary journey
into a sacred journey, a pilgrimage."

~ Phil Cousineau, The Art of Pilgrimage

As one focused on the Traveler,
    I seek the unseen threads that connect
        places,
        people, and
        moments.

Every step holds the potential
    for revelation,
    that the world is full of
    signs and wonders ~
    waiting for the traveler who moves...
        with open eyes and
        an open heart.

So, I continue on this endless road,
    a pilgrim not to a single shrine,
    but to the infinite mysteries that lie along the way.

Some roads call quietly. But they call.

A Dream, a Plan, and a Commitment ♦
Learnings from my friend, Candi

Some say a dream
    without a plan
        is just a wish.

Some say a plan
    without a commitment
        is just an idea.

I say a commitment
    without a dream
        forgets why it began.

You'll wake one day
    in a city you meant to pass through
    and wonder whose life
        you've been living.

Or, you'll find your calendar full
    and your compass quiet.
That's when you'll feel it -
    the ache for something you never named.

Guard your dream.
    Let it breathe.
    Let it change.
    Don't let it vanish
        beneath what seems practical,
        beneath what others call it,
        beneath what you think is urgent.

Think about that
    the next time a journey stirs in you.
Or the next time you call something
    a destination.

When We Both Say Yes ♥
Travels With a Muse

We met in another time -
    in this life,
    young enough to know the look
    and old enough to stay on our paths.

Years later, our paths crossed again -
    like a place I'd imagined for years
    but never dared to visit.

"There's a ship," you said.
    The idea hung between us
    like a door we'd never opened.

I'd traveled alone before,
    most of my life
    carried my own silence,
    made my own mistakes.

But, I longed for 'together'
    for sharing
    for connection
    for exploring
    for waking next to her in a foreign port
    for hearing a language new to her
    for seeing the same thing anew in her eyes

But this -
    this was offering to share
    the self I only knew in motion
    with the one who breathed life into it
        and into me.

"Yes," I said,
    not to the itinerary,
    but to discovering
    who we might become
    when the world is new to both of us.

"Yes," you echoed,
    and something shifted –
    not just in our plans,
    but in the space between us.

There was the airport bar,
    where you posed for me
    like the lady in the photo.

Except, in that brief stopover,
    you looked more elegant than
    anyone had the right to in a photo,
    or on a layover.

Now we stand at the port,
    bags at our feet,
    the ship waiting.

We've said yes to more than a cruise –
    we've said yes to seeing
    who we are when the world
    opens its arms to both of us.

We step aboard,
    travelers in each other's story,
    ready to discover
    what waits to be found.

The Weight of a Ticket ♦

It seems simple ~
    a slip of paper,
    a QR code,
    a confirmation number.

But this isn't **just a ticket**.

It's a promise to myself,
    a continued step toward a dream,
    a continued leap into the unknown.

Each ticket holds a question:
    What will I discover?
    Who will I meet?
    Who will I become?

And when the wheels leave the ground,
    the wait was worth it, and
    the weight disappears ~
        into freedom.

The Best Wrong Turn ♥
(A missed flight to Pittsburgh)

The groan was involuntary ‑
    the kind that comes when plans unravel.
    The board flashed **CANCELLED**.
    Not delayed. Not rescheduled. Cancelled.

I wasn't the only one.
    She stood at the counter,
        fingers tapping the edge,
        calm but calculating.

Another reroute, another inconvenience.
    A sideways glance.
    A quiet exchange.

    Her flight ‑ also cancelled.
    Same destination. Same detour.

I invited her for a drink at an airport bar.
    She hesitated ‑ just for a beat ‑ then smiled,
        tilting her head, she *already knew where this was going.*

By the time we landed,
    Pittsburgh wasn't just a conference stop,
    but a city painted in her laughter,
    at the hotel bar,
    in the way she absently stirred her martini,
    fingers playing with the bamboo olive stick ‑
        or was it anticipation itself?

The weekend unfolded like an unplanned itinerary,
    each **moment** a **detour** we didn't know we needed.

        Some flights take you where you planned to go.
        Some take you where you were meant to be.

35

Dreaming in Tandem ♥
When Tomorrow Can't Come Fast Enough

We were kids,
    barely knew each other
    professionals, but piqued
    alone, but unafraid.

"Florence first," you said, "Then Venice. Two nights."
    "What if we stay longer?" I countered.
    "What if we never come back?"

We talked through
    the layover in London,
    Pisa to Florence by train,
    our single bags holding everything
    we'd need to become new versions of ourselves.

"Tell me again about the David," you'd whisper.
    "Tell me about the gondolas," I'd answer back.
    Each conversation adding weight
        to a trip that felt too good to be real.

The anticipation became
    its own destination, each conversation
    building with the intensity and passion
    we were aching to live.

We asked friends where to eat
    found the ones we could afford -
        places tucked away
        for pasta and wine.

Our hotel in Florence
    became romantic in our imaginations -
    not luxury, but ours.

A place to fall asleep exhausted from wonder,
    a place to stay awake all night,
    a place to wake up and ask,
        "Where should we get lost today?"

I imagined
    your face when you saw
    the David for the first time,
    the way you'd grab my arm
    and whisper something
        just for me.

You dreamed of gondolas
    and getting lost,
    of morning coffee
    in St. Mark's Square
    while the city woke up.

We promised each other
    things we'd do,
    places we'd see,
    moments we'd create -
    each promise making our hearts beat faster.

And somewhere between
    the planning and the packing,
    I realized
    we just weren't counting down to Italy.

We were anticipating
    who we'd become
    when the world
    was new to both of us.

Ode of the Missed Connection ♥
... *On My Last Trip With Her*

There's always a moment ~
  just before a suitcase zips,
  just after the sky goes
  purple at the edge ~
when you wonder
if this is the last time
you'll see each other
in this way.

We said that once
  in the mountains.
Another time, more quietly
  on a breeze-heavy street
  near the ocean,
  when the jazz was
  too good to interrupt
  and the silence
  was already answering
  the question.
Twice on road trips.

You were my compass
  that never pointed north.

You pointed to trouble,
  to art markets before sunrise,
  to alleys that smelled like
    cinnamon and gasoline,
  to beds with
    too many stories
    not enough hours
    not enough sleep
    just holding.

You were the map
I folded wrong on purpose.
The detours I never
  regretted.

Even through our last sailing,
  you felt it.
Something in the way I stood
  you said
as if the ocean had a secret
  you were finally
  ready to hear
  without me.
We laughted and
  held each other.

Too close for strangers.
Too polite for lovers.
Too late for repair.

That night,
the moon came out
looking like it had missed
  something too.

Now,
I scroll through
old boarding passes
like love letters in code.

I find your happiness
  tucked into
the background noise
of our restaurant in Pisa.

38

I feel your presence
   in the spaces between
   the words in
   my unfinished books.

I find my own shadow
   thinner in every picture
   without you.

I miss you.
   Not just the you that
   traveled with me.
   But the me that arrived
   only when you did...

   The conversant me.
   The touching me.
   The poetic me.

The one who kissed you
   without worrying
   about where we'd land.

Instead,
   the inconsistent one,
   the wandering one,
   the closed-lipped one
   was the one who boarded.

And maybe that's what
   a **missed connection** is ~
   not the one you didn't get,
   but the one you got once,
   held in both hands,
   and let go anyway.

Some people you meet
are like flights in the night~
   no boarding call,
   no destination,
   just a sudden hush
   as the air changes,
   and for a moment
   you think you
should've been on it.

Others,
you spend your life
   trying to make;
   running
   to your gate time,
   only to arrive
as the doorway closes
   after the jetbridge
   is pulled back
   from the plane.

You were both.

And I
   was always
just a step too far behind.

THE SPACE BETWEEN YES AND GO

*Sometimes the truth depends
on a walk around the lake.*

~ David Whyte

Clarity doesn't always arrive with the decision ~ it brews in the silence after and before. There is still that "space between."

The decision is made. The ticket is booked. The path is chosen. But before departure, there is a peculiar kind of stillness ~ an in-between space where time seems to hesitate, stretching itself between anticipation and reality.

Waiting is not passive.

It is filled with silent preparations, second-guessing, excitement, and the slow, steady hum of time pulling us forward. It is the place where imagination runs wild ~ where the journey exists only in our minds, untarnished by reality.

> ~ Is anticipation part of the journey, or a test of patience?
> ~ How does waiting shape how we experience the journey?
> ~ What is in the space between deciding and departing?

This is the moment when the world holds its breath, and we do too ~ standing at the threshold, knowing that soon, everything will change.

SECTION 3

WHEN TIME HOLDS ITS BREATH

BETWEEN HERE AND HERE

"Waiting is not mere empty hoping.
It has the inner certainty of reaching the goal."

\- The I Ching

The quiet period before the leap.

Waiting is the traveler's pause, the moment between intention and action. The bags may be packed, the itinerary set, but time seems to stretch, meandering at its own pace. It's a frustrating and profound space-a chance to reflect on what lies ahead while savoring the anticipation of every thought.

In this waiting, we understand that travel is more than motion. It's preparation for change. Each second spent imagining the journey deepens its meaning, turning even the silence before departure into something sacred.

Patience is a traveler's virtue, for in the pause lies possibility. To wait well is to ready the soul for the adventure, ensuring that when the door finally opens, we step through not as the person who waited but as the one who was prepared to begin.

3 AM ☻ ♦

3 AM, night before departure:
> Eyes wide, mind racing,
>> Did I pack the charger?
>> Cancel the mail?
>> Where is my passport?
> A light somewhere else seems too bright.
> The ceiling fan mocks my sleeplessness.

3 AM, airport floor in Chicago:
> Tornado warning.
>> Flight cancelled, gates closed,
>> Alyssa curled against brother,
>>> using her jacket as a blanket,
>>> strangers snore in chorus.
> The janitor's mop bucket wheels squeak.

3 AM, somewhere over Colorado:
> The redeye's cruel mathematics,
>> too tired to sleep,
>> too wired to rest,
>> watching strangers' heads loll
>> in the blue glow of screens.
> The flight attendant's footsteps
> echo through pressurized dreams.

3 AM, hotel room in Prague:
> Jet lag's revenge,
>> ceiling staring back at me,
>> where am I?
>> wondering what day it is.
> The city sleeps outside my window
> while my memory keeps me awake.

3 AM, waiting for the Uber that said 2:30:
Standing on a corner in Bangkok,
phone battery at 12%,
wondering if I'll become one of those stories
people tell about travelers who vanished.
The street dogs know something I don't
about patience.

3 AM, train through Romania:
Sitting upright, neck cramped,
the conductor's flashlight
sweeping through my dreams,
tickets checked by ghosts
who speak in rubber stamps
and tired sighs.

3 AM, phone ringing in Hong Kong:
"Did I wake you?"
Mom's voice, confused by math
she'll never quite master.
"No, Mom. It's tomorrow here.
Or yesterday. I'm not sure anymore."
Time zones are relationship assassins.

3 AM, cruise ship cabin:
She stares at her phone,
reading the text again:
"Mom, I'm in the hospital,
heart issues."
She's floating somewhere.
The ocean doesn't care
about a mother's panic.
She's beautiful.

3 AM, first night home:
>Body confused, heart heavy,
>>missing the weight of unfamiliarity,
>>the comfort of being uncomfortable,
>>wondering why I ever left.
>My own bed feels like
>>the unfamiliar..

3 AM, emergency room in New York:
>Food poisoning from 2 AM streetfood
>>I was happy to find something
>>which should have been a sign.
>I speak panic,
>>we communicate in pointing and groaning.

3 AM, lost in Venice:
>Every bridge looks the same,
>>every canal calm
>>like I should be.
>No phone; no GPS
>I walk in circles
>>that might be squares.

3 AM is travel's truth-telling hour,
>when the romance strips away
>and you're left with the raw fact:
>You are very far from everything
>>you've ever called home.

It's the hour when distance
>becomes a weight in your chest,
>when time zones turn into
>an emotional mess never untangled.

But 3 AM also teaches
  the deepest lesson of travel:
  You are stronger
    than you ever imagined.
  You can sleep on airport floors.
  You can navigate unfamiliar hospitals.
  You can wait for rides that may never come
    and still find your way.

Somehow,
  in that dark hour
  when you feel most alone,
  you discover that
  you are the you and
  you are the companion
  you've been waiting for.

3 AM is when you learn
  that home isn't a place –
  it's the courage
  to be yourself
  anywhere in the world,
  even when the world
  feels impossibly far
  from everything
  you've ever known.

Besides, it's 3 AM somewhere in the world.

The Weight of Waiting ☻

I. The Time Warp
Time doesn't just slow in airports ~
    it becomes thick, sticky,
    pressing against your chest
    It has been 1:47 PM for an hour.

In this *pergatory*
    between here and there,
    we all become time travelers,
    trapped in waiting.

II. The Ritual of Waiting
I check my phone: 2:47 PM
I check the gate screen: DELAYED
I check my boarding pass: Seat 88E
I check the coffee line and wonder,
    "Do I really need another bad coffee?"

III. The Cast of Characters
The cast of characters unfolds:
    A child screams.
    The Red Bull runner sprints.
    The professional snorer drones.
    The eternal nail-clipper clicks.
    I feel like a human origami

IV. The False Hope
The muffled apology hits like a wet rag ~
    robotically indifferent.
Something about missing a pilot, an engine,
    or the plane itself. Cancel the flight.

The audience, because it more like a show now, moans

V. The Philosophical Turn

Then, a miracle:
> **The gate agent speaks real words.**
> My muscles unknot,
> > the wave of humanity stirs,
> Yes, there is an afterlife!

Other than the shopping mall and food court
airports are not the homerun of patience.

But truth is:
> we're all just practicing
> the art of existing
> between here and there,
> learning to find meaning
> in moments that stretch eternal.

And the longest hour starts again ~
> on the way home,
> when you've learned
> to surrender with a soggy donut,
> grace, and maybe a smile.

51

Queue Culture ☻

The queue:
    a living, breathing organism of barely contained rage,
    fed by frustration and bound by unspoken rules
    that everyone knows but no one taught us.

We **shuffle forward,**
    I practice the ancient art
    of existing in someone else's personal space
    without losing my mind.
    The TSA officer watches,
        their expression the picture of practiced indifference,
        and the meaning of "personal item."

At Customs, the queue stretches endlessly,
    suspicion and passport stamps abound.
    We practice our answers:
        "Vacation,"
        "Business,"
        "Not smuggling exotic fruit, I swear."
    The officer scans my face,
        (like in times past)
        and for a moment,
        I wonder if I really am guilty of something.

The coffee line
    is where the queue culture reaches its peak,
        coffee drinks that require a call to the help desk.
    Lena (not with me) orders
        decaf jasmine green tea
            (if they have it) or
        decaf green tea
            (if they don't) ⁓

She's definitely the safest person
    to stand behind in travel history.
Behind her: me, wanting an Americano
    and questioning life's choices that led here.

We are all equal -
    executives and backpackers,
    families and lone wolves.

Each queue has its own heartbeat,
    its own unspoken rules:
    the sacred space between bodies,
    the subtle dance of merging lines,
    the silent judgment of those
    who dare to cut ahead.

Queue culture isn't just about lines -
    it's about endurance;
    it's about finding grace in the waiting;
    it's about learning to **laugh at the absurdity of life**,
    and, standing behind the guy in the wrong security line.

As I reach the front, at last, I realize life itself is one big queue, a wavy line of hopes and detours, leading us toward the moments that matter.

Through a Child's Eyes 😊
(Overheard on planes, trains, and a car trip)

"Are we there yet?"
"How much longer?"
"Wait ~ what's that over there?!"

The questions come in waves,
    a chorus of curiosity and impatience,
    as their minds race ahead of our journey.

They're glued to the window on an airplane.
    They point out the clouds,
        imagining dragons and castles,
        they name the red cars we pass
        or the ones racing us to nowhere.

Their excitement becomes contagious.

The world is large through their eyes,
    each stop an adventure,
    each turn a discovery.

They remind us~
    travel isn't about the destination;
    it's about seeing with wonder
    and asking,
        "What's next?"

Ode to My Quiet Compass ♦
for Johanna

You've traveled through more chaos –
    from chip crumbs hurled like hail in Oslo
    to Vienna Sausage dinners
    beneath the sun at midnight in Stockholm
    and an overnight flight to Chile for a day trip.

You never asked for these miles,
    yet you carried them with a dry wit,
    and the kind of patience
    only a daughter could lend
    to a father wandering
    half by instinct, half by guess.

    "Dad, if the pilot needs to know my weight...
    maybe that's a sign we just shouldn't go."

Fair enough. We went anyway.
    Early flight: Dallas to Anchorage.
    We drove: Anchorage to Kenai.
    A 6-seat plane: Kenai to GodKnowsWhere, orca circling.
    A fishing boat with fish guts on the floor to somewhere,
        wind in your hair, your little rollaboard behind you.
    We ended at a cabin with no hot water, no power,
        and no forgiveness if I forgot batteries.

We learned 'travel' originates from '**travail.**'
    Makes sense.

You met it all
    with a raised eyebrow
    that said more than
    any travel journal ever could.

P.S. She travels still, just not *my* way.

Spreadsheet Love ♦ ☻
=DedicatedTo(Nicole & HerMagic)

```
=IF(Life="Normal",
        "Create TripPlan.xlsx",
        "Open Vacation.xlsx")

=SET("Sheet1", {
    "To-Do",
    "Budget",
    "Packing List",
    "Souvenirs",
    "Contingency",
    "Alyssa's COVID Recovery Protocol",
    "Levi's Regret Bag Contents",
    "Matt's Notes (still pending)"})

=DEFINE("FamilyUnit",
        "Nicole & Matt & Alyssa & Levi")

=IF(FlightStatus="Canceled",
    CHANGE.MODE("Fix"),
    "RecalculateItinerary",
    "Rebook",
    "Update Spreadsheet",
    "Don't Ask Matt",
    "TextGroup: 'Guess What Happened…'")

=IF(TerminalWait>60,
    VLOOKUP("Caffeine", "ORD", 2, FALSE))

=IF(ChildMood="Meltdown",
            "Redirect with Snacks",
            "Open Sheet: Emergency")

=IF(Alyssa="Coughing + Curled Up",
        "Adjust Row: AlyssaCare",
        "RestOnMoms.Lap & Levis.shoulder")
```

```
=IF(Levi="Philosophical" or "AstroPhysics",
    CONCAT("Window Seat, ",
           "Playlist: Melancholy Calm"),
           "Sit by wing for distraction")

=REN(Memory[Unexpected], Memory[Perfect])

=IF(OR(HowFar>Comfort, TimeZone>Comfort),
     "Color-Code the Day by Energy Level",
     "Add Optional Nap Cell")

=IF(TimeZone=NUL,
    FORMAT("Wake Time",
           "Emotional Readiness"))

=IF(Anyone='Whining', ACTIVATE('The Look'),
AUTO-COMPLIANCE=TRUE)

=IF(Gate="Moved Again",
          "Assign New Path"
          "Bathroom Break",
    ANDIF(Shoes="Uncomfortable",
               "RegretChoice",
               "WalkTall"
               "LookGood"
               "KeepCalm"))

=IF("Airport Tornado Warning"=TRUE, {
     "Don't act panicky",
     "Locate tunnel",
     "Hold family tight",
     "Remember to laugh"})

=CONCATENATE(
     "Mother, Business-Owner, ",
     "Award-Winner, Life-Partner, ",
     "Ultimate-Encourager, ",
     "Planner, Dream-Giver")
```

```
=IF(TripComplete=TRUE,
   CONCAT("Remember: ",
      SUM("The strange hotel pillows",
          "The laugh at the closed museum",
          "The airport floor stories")),
   "Begin new spreadsheet")

=RETURN(Wonder)
```

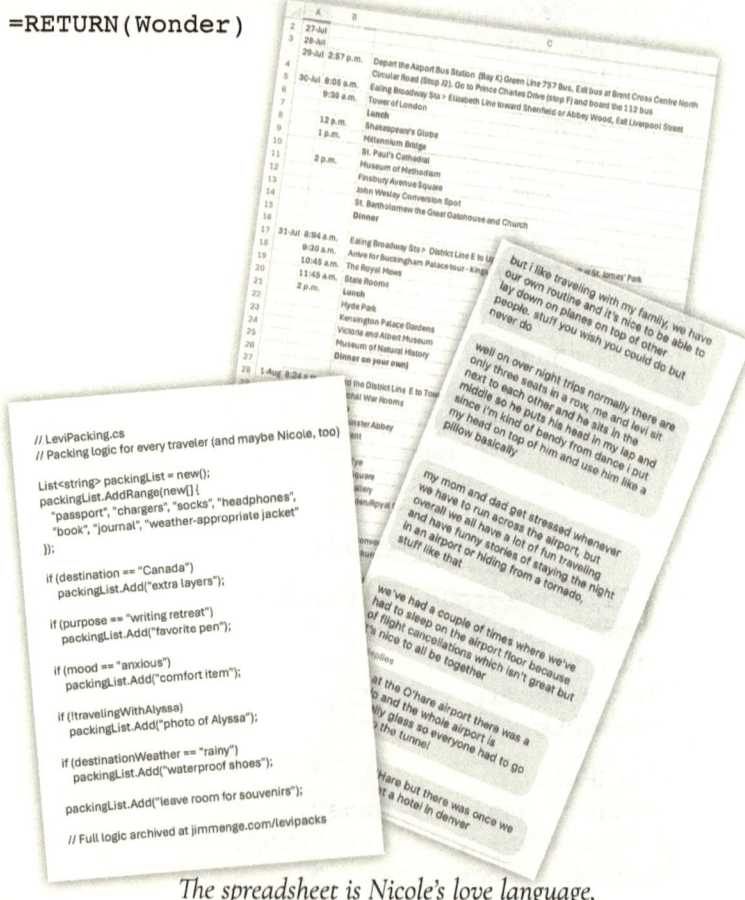

The spreadsheet is Nicole's love language,
and her family speaks it fluently.

Be Patient, Wait Mindfully ♦
Lessons in Slowing Down

Travel is not a race;
  it's a breath, one full cycle at a time.
Be still. **Become aware.**

Hear the baby cry at 5 a.m.,
  the gate and flight announcements,
  the shuffle of shoes in the boarding line.
Every sound **a prelude, an opening note in your story.**

Feel the hunger pangs in an unfamiliar city,
  the warmth of sunlight on your skin,
  the weight of your well-traveled bag against your side.

Smell the unfamiliar ~
  a bakery at dawn,
  a forest after the rain,
  the spices and flowers of a market alive.

Taste what's offered:
  the sweetness of a ripe mango,
  the bitter tang of coffee brewed just right,
  the salt in the air when you stand near the sea.

Look, truly look ~
  a city skyline emerging through the clouds,
  the hush before a Sedona sunset,
  even a crowded station has a chaotic harmony.

The waiting is not an interruption;
  it is the pause between the notes.

And, in the hush between arrivals
your journey begins.

59

THE FIRST STEP, THE FIRST FLIGHT

Yes: I am a dreamer.
For a dreamer is one who can
only find his way by moonlight,
and his punishment is that he
sees the dawn before the rest of the world.

- Oscar Wilde, The Critic as Artist, 1891

The moment before departure is a threshold. A pause before what's next. The air hums with the sound of possibilities, of hesitation, of doors sliding open and closing behind.

The plane leaves the gate, lines up on the runway, and begins its takeoff roll. The point of no return. The wheels lift, the ground falls away. The waiting ends. The breath releases.

This moment has changed for me over time. The first time I left, I didn't know if I would find my way back. Now, I wonder if I will recognize the one who returns.

- What is it that truly begins when we depart?
- What we can learn about our self we thought we knew?
- What do we carry with us that we don't want to carry back?

This step is a letting go. A surrender to something unseen ~ something that already knows the way. Time, which held its breath in waiting rooms and queues, finally exhales. The journey inward begins.

Beyond this moment lies the real journey ~ not the one measured in miles, but the one that creates possibilities of who we are.

This is where we stop being tourists of the outward ~
and begin the real journey inward.

61

SECTION 4

WHY THE JOURNEY CHANGES US

Derick Lowe: Where writing and wandering meet
(with special appearance by Bev Warburton in the window)

THE JOURNEY WRITES ITSELF

*"You do not travel if you are afraid of the unknown;
you travel for the unknown that reveals you to yourself."*

~ Ella Maillart, Swiss Adventurer

What we surrender to in that first step is what matters ~

To travel is to transform, to step into the world's unfolding narrative. It is a **gate swarm of movement and stillness** ~ every sense awakened, every moment savored, every emotion revealed. Traveling is the **heart of the traveler's odyssey**, where each step writes another line in the epic of their life.

Finally, the moment arrives. The trip begins.

And let's be honest, it's rarely perfect. Unless, like me, you **revel in every line** at airports and Starbucks, **cramped and middle plane seats**, **train delays**, **computer glitches**, **schedule changes**, and the **chaos of customs interrogations**.

Perhaps you have a soft spot for strange hotel pillows, buffet roulette, or sweating through every season in Kuala Lumpur.

Or maybe you enjoy the **little surprises** ~ like mistaking someone else's plane seat for your own, or hearing your name shouted across a crowded airport when you were sure no one knew you were there. Or, worse, realizing someone does.

Because the world is smaller than we think.

But maybe this isn't the point.

Not perfection, but participation. Not control, but surrender. The unstraight journey changes us. Staying in an ancient Moorish home in Seville with all of its deep blue colors, Arabic arches and spiraling staircases makes one feel like they were there hundreds of years earlier.

We become more flexible, more forgiving, more curious. We find who we truly are when we travel. We become fellow travelers on the Camino pilgrimage, share a meal with a stranger in an Indonesian restaurant in Amsterdam on a business trip, and help a lost traveler at Penn Station.

The delays teach patience. The wrong turn sparks creativity. The lost luggage? Perspective. The missed train? Flexibility. The unexpected kindness of strangers? Gratitude. These become the landmarks of our journey experiences.

~

So go.

Embrace the imperfections.

In the end,
    the journey writes itself.

And perhaps,
    the journey rights us, too.

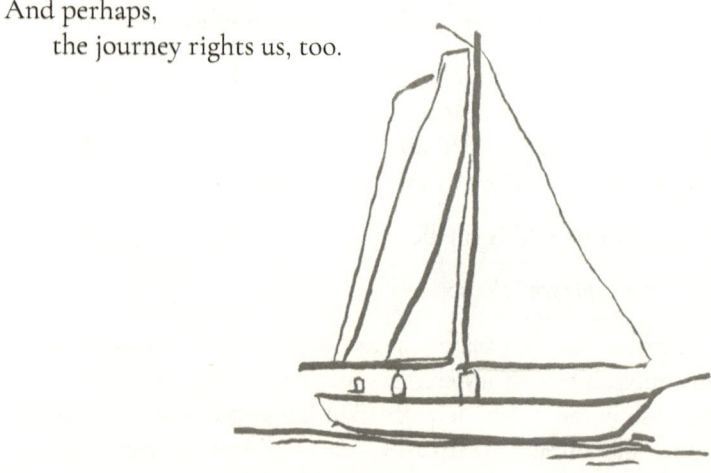

The Scent of a City ♦
Lessons in Slowing Down

Some cities introduce themselves
　　through their landmarks.
　　Others greet you first by their scent.

New York smells like ambition -
　　steam from subway grates,
　　a hotdog cart wafting mustard and onions.

Jakarta is adventure -
　　thick with curry, warm spice, and traffic.
　　mixing with monsoon rain on hot concrete.

Kuala Lumpur sticks to the skin -
　　human, pulsing, alive,
　　with durian that follows you home.

Sapporo - where the air cuts clean -
　　even the cold carries a scent,
　　like breathing through crystal.

Penn Station smells like movement -
　　trains, urgency, leather, heels clicking
　　people brushing past one another.

Some cities taste better than they look,
　　some linger on the skin.

And some,

*you remember best when you close your eyes
breathing them back to life one scent at a time.*

67

Travel: Two Voices In My Head ♦ ☺

The dream	*wide awake*
The discovery	*the world is bigger than me*
The decision	*burn the map*
The pause	*heartburn, hesitation, or hunger?*
The going	*and still, I'm not ready*
The return	*"Welcome back!" But, who returned?*

The return to the dream	*wide awake, again*

Traveling is not the end.	*some travel never ends.*

It is the beginning –	*It is the addiction–*
into the unknown,	*a needle in the vein of routine*
a new story.	*each steps rewrites your DNA*

Returning changed,	*rearranged*
collecting places	*... and leaving pieces of myself behind*

Still arguing over window or aisle.

When the World Felt Like Home ♥

There is travel, and then there is belonging.

Not on the itinerary, not in the guidebooks -
    just an open door,
    a shared meal,
    a seat on the tatami.

Churrascaria pulled me into its smoky world,
    where conversation and fire-grilled meat
    stretched deep into the night.

There are places that envelope me
    places that swallow me whole,
    but with a home where goats were the landscape.

Where broken animals and I nursed each other
    back into something like whole.

Yom Kippur while the Miami skyline thundered.
Sushi and Asahi while Tokyo's last train disappeared.
Tapas in Seville before horses stormed the arena.
Singapore, where family ate with us after our workday.
Athens, where everyone pulls up a chair like blood.
Iceland, we shed clothes and secrets in the geothermal water.

Dragged through a parade, but lunch after
    in the desert of San Pedro de Atacama

There are places you visit.
And there are places that take you in,
    even just for a moment.

These are the places that live in your bloodstream,
that call your name in other people's accents".

69

The Breaking Point ◆

The Camino is a road walked by millions,
　　but the only footprints that matter are your own.

I had walked for fourteen days
　　through villages that whispered with history,
　　along paths that carried pilgrims for a thousand years.
Blood and blisters on my feet,
　　exhaustion in my bones,
　　loneliness pressing in.

The journey had become a battle ~ not against the road,
　　but against the voice that whispered, **"Stop"**.
I had come so far, but the final stretch
　　just three more days felt impossible.
I sat at a bus stop, defeated,
　　I cried, not from pain, but from something deeper.

What is it about the Camino that does this?
Why does it break you before it rebuilds you?

Shirley MacLaine walked this road,
　　searching for past lives, tracing the echoes of souls.
　　"Listen to the sounds beyond silence."

Martin Sheen's son wrote him a movie, **The Way**,
　　grief turned into footsteps, loss turned into miles.
　　　"Don't choose a life, dad. Live one."

Paulo Coelho made it a metaphor,
　　a path not just across Spain, but into the self.
　　　"I dedicated most of my life to penetrate the 'secrets'
　　　　of the universe..."

For a thousand years, pilgrims walked with their burdens...
    seeking healing, redemption, revelation.
I wasn't sure what I was seeking,
    but I knew this:
        the only way out was forward.

An hour later, I stood up.
    One foot, then the other.
        One step, then another.

Sometimes, the hardest part of the journey
    is convincing yourself to take the next step.

But what if the breaking point is just a threshold?
A moment **not of surrender**,
    but of **becoming**?

      "Try not to resist the changes that come your way.
      Instead, let life live through you."

                    ~ Rumi

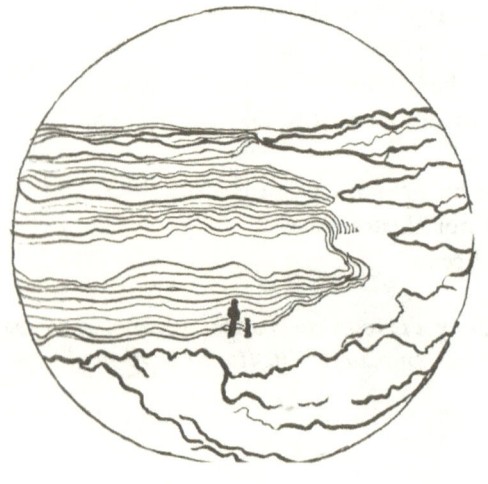

Moving ♦

Laguna Beach, What the Waves Spoke

To falter is to feel.
To feel is to question.
To question is to awaken.
To awaken is to begin.

To wait is to watch life retreat
    like a tide that forgets your name.

To dive is to return to yourself –
    through breath, through fear,
    through the silence that shaped you.

To trust is to lean forward
    into the unknown
    as if it already loves you.

To rise is to remember
    the weight was never yours to keep.

To breathe is to unshackle
    each chain disguised as thought,
    each shadow mistaken for truth.

To move is holy.

And you –
    you owe nothing to what broke you
    you've already outrun the ghosts
    you are not done becoming
    your scars are your wings.

Go,
    the sky is waiting.

Revelations on the Road ♦

Moscow swallowed me whole.
    Not just in size but in significance ~
        as if I could vanish between one footstep and the next.
    It is one thing to be alone.
    It is another to cease to exist.

In **Cancún**, my body staged a revolt.
    A heart attack, time hemorrhaging faster than blood.
    Racing death to the border,
        realizing mortality packs light ~
        it follows you everywhere.

In **Santiago**, the weight of empty pockets.
    No money, no escape route,
        watching the world spin past
        while I stood still as stone.
    Understanding that the world moves on,
        whether or not you have the means to move with it.

Old Havana, lost in the past.
    Where a stranger behind the wheel
        drove me past the point of no return
        parked at a fortune tellers rum-smelled porch
            where I was not prepared to hear what she said.

Travel strips away the illusion of certainty
    it teaches you that vulnerability is the price of admission,
    that discovery and destruction
    share the same coordinates.

Some places teach you about the world.
Others remind you what it means to be human.

                I have been to both.
                I have survived both.

Unexpected Intersections ♦

A missed bus, a delayed flight,
    I stumbled into a **conversation**.

Atlanta airport, travels with a colleague
    a stranger with no home ~
    a **shared laugh** over airport chicken.
    Three lives briefly crossing,
       then vanishing back into motion.

A train threading the California coast ~
    Fred (my brother) and I **trading life lessons**
    with bikers from God-knows-where,
    our laughter louder than the tracks.

In a bustling Istanbul market,
    a shopkeeper **poured us tea**.
    "On the house," she said.
    We left without the rug,
       but the tea stayed with me for days.

At the Hong Kong ferry terminal,
    a toddler caught my gaze,
    and turned my connection into **peekaboo**.
    Even the businessman beside me paused ~
       his briefcase forgotten, his smile intact.

These moments remind me ~
    travel isn't just about the places.

    It's the **people**,
       the fleeting **sparks**,
       the unplanned **collisions**,

and the stories we carry away.

The Art of Being Lost ☻

In **Paris**, I ordered a café au lait.
    The waiter smirked. "Ah, an American?"
I nodded. He brought me an espresso. Liquid disappointment.

In **Tokyo**, I bowed too low,
    confusing reverence with politeness.
The old shopkeeper bowed lower. I bowed back. Ugh.

In **Buenos Aires**, I tried my best Spanish.
    "Una cerveza, por favor."
The bartender handed me two. Then joined me.

In **Istanbul**, I nodded
    when I should've shaken my head.
I left with a Turkish romance novel purely for research.

In **Bangkok**, I pointed at a menu,
    hoping for something mild.
Three bites in, I saw my ancestors. For three days.

In **Amman**, I haggled with confidence.
    The vendor grinned.
I paid double for the experience. Twice.

In **Berlin**, I asked for directions.
    A kind stranger answered – in perfect English.
I walked the wrong way, and met her at a bar.
She smiled, "I hoped you'd got lost."

Sometimes, words fail.
    Sometimes, gestures mislead.
    Sometimes, meaning just goes missing.

**Sometimes, I'm just a wandering
human translation error.**

But there's another kind of lost ~
 the kind that strips away more than language,
 more than direction,
 more than the illusion of competence.

In Venice,
 I turned a corner, then another,
 and suddenly, every canal looked the same.
 "Is that the same gondola?"
  No, all of gondoliers wave.
  And laugh. And point.
 At the beautiful confusion of tourists
  who think they know where they're going.

In Rhodes,
 My father's 8mm silent films
  chasing a goat for fun, then
  seeing the goat slaughtered and hung from a tree
  then roasted.
 Old, leathery men playing backgammon
  drinking sludge-for-coffee.
 "Which way to the village?"
  The Yaya pointed down three streets,
  yelling in rapid Greek.
 I got lost anyway.

In Istanbul
 the Grand Bazaar spun me like a dervish.
 Every stall looked like the last ~
  rugs, lamps, spices.
  "Have I been here before?"
  A day later,
   I left with a book a tourist left behind
   and a stall seller sold me that I didn't need.

In the Atacama
    I wandered into an Easter parade,
        wearing sleeping shorts
        with a splitting headache
        lassoed as Diablo.
    "Why am I here?"
        I wasn't sure if I should escape,
            or start plotting my sainthood.

By the time I reached Shanghai and Beijing,
    Bucharest and Budapest, São Paulo and Saint Paul,
    Austria and Australia, Sydney NSW and Sydney NS,
        it didn't matter anymore.

Being lost wasn't a problem to solve.

The lost traveler learns the hardest lesson:
    you are not in control.
    And that's exactly where wisdom begins.

Some arts can't be unlearned.
    But maybe that's the point.
    Every traveler eventually discovers:
        we don't master the art of navigation.
    We master the art of being lost
        with grace, with curiosity,
        and occasionally, with laughter.

Because in the end,
    the best discoveries happen
    when we stop pretending
    we know where we're going
    and start trusting
    where we're being led.

The Unexpected Journey ◆

I set out thinking we knew the way.
   A map in hand.
   An itinerary starred.
   A destination, or a lover, in mind.

...Or, did I?
Maybe I just
liked the excuse of
"unexpected."

But the road is never just the road.
   It bends when we expect it to run straight.
   It vanishes mid-sentence like a missed kiss.
   It leads us to goat parades, rooftop bars,
      or a stranger who orders me local wine
      without asking my name.

... Intentional
detours
taste like
fate with
lime and salt.

And sometimes,
   that is where the real journey begins.

Finally..!

When a missed connection becomes a night
   in a city I only stopped in for lunch;
when a wrong turn leads to a view
   I never knew we needed;
when the detour becomes the story
   I tell over candlelight to someone new.

Totally unexpected.
Totally worth it.
Totally a wrong bus.
Totally a right story.

The best journeys are never the ones we plan.
   They are the ones that change our plans.
   That rewrite us mid-sentence.

Even when we
can forsee the
unforseen.

The road, it turns out,
   has a few desires of its own.

Sometimes just
tacos at midnight.

And maybe the map was never wrong,
   only smaller than the world.
The ink stops where wonder begins.

Totally lost.
Totally alive.
The road has
jokes too.

Occasionally, we align.

Or, collide

The World Became Smaller ◆

Each generation faced its own horizons.

My mother, born in Greece
    just after the Ottomans left ~
  her ancestors
        walked from Syria and Lebanon,
        carrying stories in their pockets.
My father's people, German stock,
    crossed oceans with nothing
  but stubborn hope.

First, we walked.
    My mother's ancestors on foot, caravan perhaps,
    my father's from Hamburg to Ellis Island.
Every mile earned with blood and salt,
    blisters mapping bloodlines across continents.
At the speed of a step.

    ...the world was over there.

Then, we rode.
    Faster, farther, heavier
    Donkeys and mules carrying the loads
      over rough rocky mountain trails
    Speed came with a price
      broken bones
      exhaustion
      fear
      heat and storms.
At the speed of a hoof.

    ...the world grew closer.

Eventually, we embarked.
A train. A ship.
Growing pains.
Loose schedules.
Waiting at hotels that weren't home.
Hopes dashed.
At the speed of engines and waves -
    carpetbags in hand, uncertainty
ahead;

    ...the world became within reach.

Today, we board.
A reservation.
An app.
An air-conditioned jet bridge.
Protected from the elements.
A complaint about legroom.
Distance dissolved into an inconvenience.
At the speed of jets -
    clean, efficient, sterile.

    ...the world became familiar.

My mother carried the Ottoman Empire
    in her memories.
I carry her stories in my phone.

The world shrank to the size of a screen -
    Did we expand,
    or just learn to forget
    the weight of distance?

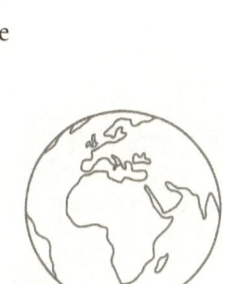

Your Journey's Exclamation Points ♦

We remember journeys not for every step,
    but for the moments that shock and awe,
    and the final breath that burns itself into us.

Psychologist Daniel Kahneman's *Peak-End Theory*
    cuts through the crap...
        The most intense experiences and the way we conclude
        them become the story we tell ourselves we lived.

Let the end of your trip be unforgettable:
    a hole-in-the-wall eatery where the chef's stories
        are the seasoning in the dish;
    a winding road to nowhere that fills you with forever;
    an impromptu street jam session halting your movement;
    the rhythm that makes your skin pulse.

These are more than experiences;
    these are the exclamation points of your journey,
    marking where the unforgettable begins and stories form.

Exhausted, worn, tried, spent;
    January, my heart as cold as outside
        after the frozen echo of justice in Oslo.
    Tears, bruises, and enveloping darkness ~
        I fled into the unknown.

For in the end,
    it is not the itinerary we remember,
    but how our heart felt
    when the journey ripped itself away.

The Inner Wonderer ☺
... With Inner Dialog

There are maps made of cities, — *London*
    maps made of moments, — *Paris*
    maps I left in the hotel room. — *Cancun*

This is not a journey of miles, — *Camino*
    but missed turns, lost passwords, — *Greece*
    gut feelings I should've listened to. — *Moscow, twice*

Each place in these pages — *Especially the spaces*
    claims to mark something profound ~ — *Chaos*
    a shift in presence or perception — *Macau bungee jump*

Some roads are well-trodden. — *Las Vegas*
Some fake confidence. — *Los Angeles*
Some remember your footsteps
    before you even show up. — *New Orleans*
Some sensually personal — *Barcelona*
Some disappear when you commit. — *Going back*
Some wait for your worst shoes. — *Florence*

This is not a travel guide. — *That's by Rick Steves*
It's a breadcrumb from someone who — *Your ex's texts*
    wandered off the main path,
    got distracted by a cheese plate — *Never Travel in a*
    and decided to call it meaning. — *Straight Line book*

Follow it lightly. — *Sedona*
No promises. — *Las Vegas (again)*
Read with one eyebrow raised. — *Casablanca*
Let the familiar stay stubborn. — *Your hometown*
Let the unknown explain itself. — *Casablanca whispers*
Expired passport. — *Greece*

And if you find yourself in these pages ~ — *Ugh*
    well, I'll make room. — *Seat 34A*

The Traveler's Path
A Journey of Inner Expansion

THERE ARE FIVE KINDS OF PLACES TO WHICH

WE TRAVEL. EACH TEACHES US SOMETHING

DIFFERENT ABOUT WHAT IT MEANS TO BE

HUMAN.

THIS IS A JOURNEY THROUGH THEM ALL - FROM

THE CROWDED TO THE SACRED, FROM THE

FAMILIAR TO THE IMPOSSIBLE.

UNKNOWN
We arrive at the edge of the map.

▲

UNFAMILIAR
We drift into what we cannot name.

▲

KNOWN
We seek what we think we know.

▲

FAMILIAR
We return to what we remember.

▲

TRODDEN
We walk where many have walked.

Travel to the Trodden ☻ ♦

The road here is paved in postcards.
    I arrive not with wonder,
        but with a checklist.

Rome, the Colosseum
Granada, the Alhambra
London, the Abbey
Machu Picchu, the ruins
New York, Katz' Deli
Even Paris ~
    places I have seen
    long before I ever saw them.

The crowd has become part of the architecture,
    elbows nudging history,
    selfie sticks rising like antennae
    trying to catch a signal from the past.

I try to feel something profound
    while dodging a Segway tour
    and someone named Gary
    explaining loudly why
    the Mona Lisa is "smaller than expected."

And yet ~
    the glass pyramid outside still catches the sunlight
The limestone entrance still holds warmth
    like it remembers something
    we've forgotten.

While visiting the Vatican,
    a boy plays flute for coins that never come.
    I find a quiet bench behind the basilica.
Not a soul with a guidebook in sight.

An old woman lights a candle
    and for a moment ~
    only the sacred breathes.
    She shows me something
        no tour guide knows:
        how to stand still
        in a place worn smooth by millions,
        and still find God
        in the spaces between footsteps.

Even here,
    where the path is packed and polished,
    my feet can still find sacred ground.

And if I listen past the noise,
    the ancient stones remember their first purpose:
    not to be seen,
    but to shelter the seeking.

And once, in stillness,
    I thought I heard the place whisper ~
        not in words,
        but in waiting.

The trodden path may be crowded,
    but it still leads somewhere holy ~
    if I'm willing to walk it with reverence
    instead of a camera.

Some places become familiar long before we know why.

(~ intro to Travel to the Known)

Travel to the Known ◆

I have seen this place
    in books,
    in films,
    in someone else's story.

Its name carries weight before I arrive.
Its image, rehearsed in my dreams.
    Athens, the Acropolis
    Oslo, winter darkness
    Lisbon, the monument to the Adventurers
    Seville, the Moorish B&B
Cities shaped by syllables
    we've learned to pronounce with reverence.

And now,
    I am here.

It is not what I expected.
    Or perhaps, exactly what I expected.
    A theater where I know all the lines
        but hearing them spoken aloud
    still catches me off guard.

The legend wears traffic and scaffolding now,
    but beneath the construction barriers,
    something ancient breathes.

So I listen.
    To the echo in the museum stairwell
        that sounds like centuries.
    To the barkeeper's casual mention
        of the poet who drank here nightly.
    To the taxi driver's silence
        between words he doesn't need to translate.

The stones are not just old ~
 they are weary
 of being photographed
 without being witnessed.

To the woman at the café
 who said "You've been here before, haven't you?"
To the stone I sat on,
 that warmed slowly beneath me
 as if remembering how to hold a guest.

The Known asks nothing new of me.

But if I look past the guidebook,
 past the curated lighting,
 it offers something deeper:

 Not a performance ~
  but a pulse.
 Not a monument ~
  but a moment, still breathing.

And so I meet this place
 not as a collector of sights,
 but as a student
 of what endures
 when the crowds go home.

Some places become familiar
the moment you stop needing them to impress you.

(~ intro to Travel to the Familiar).

Travel to the Familiar ◆ ☺

The turn in the road
    ambushes me with memory.
    And still,
        my body remembers before my mind catches up.

Melbourne, my Greek heritage calling from a cafe
Prague, Hemingway's Bar where I learned to drink alone
Tokyo, home for six years and counting
Dublin, a pub that taught me the sound of a Guiness

This street ~
    was it five years ago?
    Ten?
I walked here once
    wearing the skin of someone I used to be.

Now I return not to retrace those footsteps,
    but to see who I've become
    in the space between then and now.

The pub is still here.
    Different barstools, same worn wood.
    Same silence pooling in the corner seat.
    The bartender's eyes flicker with recognition ~
        or maybe he just knows the look
        of someone coming home
        to a place that might not remember them back.

The Familiar doesn't greet me with fanfare.
    It sits down beside me, quietly, like an old friend
    who remembers exactly how I told the story
    and kindly ignores the version I've polished since.

The stone wall bears a new chip,
    but the same wind curves through the alley,
    carrying something I didn't know I'd left behind ~
    a younger version of my laugh,
    the weight I used to carry in my shoulders,
    the way I used to walk when I thought
    no one was watching.

I see my own footprints
    half-faded in the dust,
    leading forward and back,
    forming circles I didn't know I was walking.

I do not try to step into them.
But I honor them.

And I thank this place ~
    not because it froze in time,
    but because it held space
    for who I was
    while I figured out who I'm becoming.

Some places know you better than you know yourself.
They reveal how far you've come
without taking a single step.

(~ intro to Travel to the Unfamiliar)

91

Travel to the Unfamiliar ♦

I do not speak the words he needs.
I do not know the rules that might help him.
He nods too much,
    or not enough.
Even his smile looks misshapen with panic.

He stands on the corner of Eighth and Main,
    turning his phone like a compass that's lost its north.
His clothes say "somewhere else,"
    his posture screams "help me."

Here, he is a question
    walking upright on my familiar sidewalk.

The signs that guide my daily route
    blur into symbols in his mind.
    The air that is home to me
        is like somewhere else for him.

I watch him watch the crowd
    and wonder what he's forgotten to do ~
    or who he's forgotten to be.

Still, he walks.
One foot after foreign foot.
The rhythm uncertain,
    but honest.

I approach him slowly.
    "¿Necesita ayuda?"

His relief floods his face like sunrise.

I point toward the subway entrance,
    use my hands to show two stops,
    speak the word "hospital"
    in three different ways until recognition sparks.

A woman sells flowers from a cart nearby.
    I buy one, hand it to him,
        and watch something loosen in his shoulders.
He smiles ~
    and that becomes the day's first shelter.

The unfamiliar hums with its own order.

And slowly,
    I remember what it felt like
    to be the one who didn't belong,
    to need a stranger's kindness
    more than air.

I realize I am not guiding him
    through my city.
    I am guiding myself back
    to remembering
    what it means to be human
    in a world that speaks
    a hundred languages of lost.

The unfamiliar didn't just test me.
It turned me back toward the part of myself
still willing to be surprised.
And maybe that's the only way
we ever reach the unknown.

(~ intro to Travel to the Unknown)

Travel to the Unknown ♦

No map for this.
No border crossing.
No name to whisper at the gate.

I pack light ~
 just breath and intention.
No luggage for this journey,
 only the weight I'm ready to release.

The departure gate is my kitchen chair.
The boarding pass, a closed-eye surrender.
The destination appears
 only when I stop trying to arrive.

There are no signposts here.

Only sensations ~
 a shift in light behind my eyelids,
 a silence that speaks in frequencies
 a coherence I forgot I could feel.

It begins in the body:
 the flutter of not-knowing,
 the breath before letting go,
 the stillness before becoming.
 the moment when the familiar world
  dissolves like the runway below us.

The compass spins.
The stars offer no explanation.
And still ~ the path unfolds.

I walk by feeling.
By wonder.
By the version of myself
   I've not yet remembered.

Is it a place?
A moment?
A doorway made out of breath?

Yes,
    and also ~ no.

The Unknown is not empty.
It is full of everything
   I once feared and now welcome.

Here, I am not the traveler.
I am the traveled ~
   The journey moves through me
      like wind through an open door.

I realize I've been chasing distant horizons
when the greatest adventure was always this close ~
in the stillness between one breath and the next.

This is where all journeys lead:
not away from home, but into the unknown within.

A Place is Never One Thing ♦
Each Visit in a Spiral Inward

Through the Known Lens

I have seen these cliffs before -
    in travel magazines,
    in romantic films,
    in the dreams I rehearsed
    during grey winter mornings.
Cinque Terre carries weight before I arrive,
    its image polished by expectation.
Now I am here, and it is exactly
    what I hoped, and nothing like I imagined -
    the legend wears hiking boots and sweat now.

Through the Unknown Lens

No trail map for this journey.
I sit on the rocks at Monterosso,
watching the horizon dissolve
into something I cannot name.

Through the Trodden Lens

The hiking trail is paved in Instagram posts.
I follow the crowds to Monterosso,
    checking off villages like grocery items.
Vernazza, Corniglia, Manarola, Riomaggiore -
    each one more photographed than lived in.
Gary from Texas explains loudly
    why the gelato is "overpriced but authentic."
Yet even here, between the selfie sticks,
    the ancient terraces still catch light like prayer,
and the sea whispers stories older than tourism.

Through the Familiar Lens

The switchback trail above Manarola
        ambushes me with memory.
Two years ago, I walked this same path
        wearing the shoes of someone
I thought I knew completely.
The bench overlooking the harbor is still here,
        same weathered wood, same impossible view.
I see my own footprints in the dust of time,
        leading forward and back,
                forming circles I'm still learning to walk.

The departure gate is this moment,
        the destination appears only
        when I stop trying to arrive.

Through the Unfamiliar Lens

I am the one lost now,
        asking "Dov'è la stazione?"
        with clumsy pronunciation.
An old woman selling lemons
        draws a map on my palm,
        her kindness becoming shelter
        in the architecture of foreign syllables.
Here, I am a question mark
        walking upright through cobblestone certainty,
        learning that vulnerability
                opens doors language cannot.

THE ECHO OF DEPARTED PLACES

You were born with wings,
why prefer to crawl through life?

~ Rumi

No journey lasts forever.

Even as we wander through new streets and lose ourselves
in far - away places, the quiet tug of home is always there ~
sometimes faint, sometimes insistent, but always waiting.

We leave as one person, and we return as another.

The return is inevitable, the passport bears the same name,
but the eyes that scan familiar horizons have seen things that
cannot be unseen. The world leaves traces on us: the scent of
another city, the echo of a stranger's laughter in our minds, the
weight of new stories we don't yet know how to tell.

- Is coming home a return, or just another step forward?
- How do we carry our travels within, even after unpacking?
- What if the journey isn't over, just changing shape?

We discover that departure and arrival are not opposites
but partners in the same dance. Every goodbye carries the seed
of hello. The places we leave continue to live in us, shaping
how we see the places we're yet to go.

Home becomes not a place we return to, but a way of being we
carry forward. We realize we've been changed not just by the
destinations, but by the act of seeking them.

And so we understand:
the greatest journey isn't to somewhere else.
It's to who we become along the way.

99

SECTION 5

WHERE WE RETURN

Samsara

we travel in circles
until we realize
we were always
the center

ROUND TRIP

"You do not travel if you are afraid of the unknown;
you travel for the unknown, that reveals you to
yourself."

~ Ella Maillart, Swiss Adventurer

The Least Appreciated Part of the Journey: The Return

Returning is where the journey folds back into the self.

Every journey has two parts: the going and the coming back. But here's what most travelers miss ~ the real adventure starts when you return home.

You've walked unfamiliar streets, tasted new flavors, met strangers who became friends. You've pushed boundaries, faced fears, collected stories. But now comes the deeper question: What do you do with who you've become?

Four Dimensions of Your Return

Your homecoming isn't just about unpacking bags. It's a multi-layered transformation happening on four levels:

Physical Return - Familiar spaces, unfamiliar perspective
Emotional Return ~ Reconciling past and present selves
Inward Return ~ Discovering what travel awakened within
Renewal ~ Beginning again with new possibilities

You don't just return different ~
you return charged with possibility.

The Journey Never Truly Ends ~
It Becomes Part of Us

As T.S. Eliot wrote, *We shall not cease from exploration... And the end of all our exploring will be to arrive where we started and know the place for the first time...* true discovery often emerges from stillness, memory, and the quiet spaces within.

Our souveniers are fragments of time, tucked into memory:
- a smell of street food,
- a laugh echoing in an unfamiliar café,
- a feeling we can't quite name,
- a person who became part of your trip,
- the person you are still becoming.

These moments remind us that the journey never really ends ~ it just begins to echo differently.

Eliot reflects the profound truth that travel is transformative. **The familiar becomes extraordinary**, and the journey reshapes how we see the world and ourselves.

What Will You Do with Who You've Become?

In this section you'll discover how to:

- **Transform** travel memories into lasting wisdom
- **Navigate** the complexity of coming home changed
- **Build** on your journey as a foundation for what's next
- **Keep** the spirit of exploration alive in everyday life

Your round trip isn't complete until you've fully returned ~ not just to a place, but to yourself.

What They Taught ♦
... *What I Learned* ☻

My children taught me **wonder**, again;
> the thrill of seeing the world as endlessly surprising.
> Roughing the Alaska wilderness. Midnight lights in Oslo.

A mate shares their **perspective**;
> unveiling beauty we might have missed.
> Heavy baggage. Paris romance in cold, rainy February.

A new love **surprises** us;
> showing us the world in ways we never imagined.
> Heavy overhead bags, heels while hiking.

A lost love still **teaches** us;
> revealing what mattered most, only once it's gone.
> A middle seat, a cruise companion, sharing a glass of wine.

A stranger **changes** everything;
> teaching us that a brief moment can be **profound**.
> Road rage in Panama. Unplanned dinner for two in Lima.

A solo travel **strips** us bare;
> teaching us who we are when no one's watching.
> Wrong train in Barcelona. Right café at dawn.

Each
> fills a gap,
> shares a laugh,
> opens a door to the unexpected,

Travel reshapes us,
> not just by where we go,
> but by who we're with.

I smile,
grateful for the doors they've shown me,
and those that slammed behind me.

Tokens ♦☺

I carry pieces of the journey home with me -
    tokens of time and place, small enough to hold,
    but heavy with meaning.

A smooth stone from a Japanese riverbed,
    a frayed boarding pass on Concorde I got off eBay,
    a guitar pick from a cafe player in Sante Fe,
    a scarf from a friend in France,
        still smelling of her perfume.

These are more than objects -
    they are **fragments of memory**.

They speak of fleeting moments:
    a meditative **sunrise** over a Kyoto rooftop,
    a laughter-filled **meal** with Sapporo strangers
        who felt like family,
    a **hand held** watching the Milky Way rise.

Tokens are whispers of what we cannot hold -
    a sunset, a scent, a song,
    the way the air felt finishing the Camino.

They remind me of **who I was** in those moments:
    open-hearted, less afraid, more awake.

In their silence,
    they carry the power to take me back
    to places I'll never see again,
        yet somehow never left.

I keep them not for their price,
    but for the stories they tell,
    and the **parts of myself** they let me remember.

Because in the end,
>the most meaningful souvenirs
>don't sit on shelves, cling to the fridge, or hide in drawers.

The most meaningful souveniers are

>the moments,
>the lessons,
>the laughable missteps,
>>asking a woman directions (accidentally, to her house)
>the pieces of myselves
>>I **never expected** to find along the way.

The Traveler's Mirror ◆

Returning is *the traveler's mirror*,
    reflecting not only where we've been,
    but **who we've become**.

The Camino **return** brought me **an acknowledgment...**
A Greek monestary **return** brought an **awakening...**
The Atacama **return** brought me an **awareness**...
The Tibetan Plateau **return** brought me **awe**...

    of the ways I changed
    and the ways the world had not.

        "Farewells can be shattering,
        but returns are surely worse."
            ~Margaret Atwood, The Blind Assassin

In every journey, there is **the quiet truth**:
    that the places we leave behind
    will not remain as we remember them ~
    and neither will we.

Yet, we return,
    drawn by the hope of finding home again,
    even if home is no longer what I wished it would be.

The journey reveals not who we were, but the unseen within.

Feelings of the Return ♥
by Tricia & Joey

The Return is **bittersweet**,
    nostalgia for the adventures we've had,
    gratitude for the memories we've made,
    and a quiet ache for the places we've left behind.

There's relief in *returning to the familiar* –
    the navigation of our neighborhood
    the scent of our home,
The familiarity of our furniture,
    the warmth of our bed –

The return *isn't just an ending*;
    it's a **beginning** –
    a moment to reflect,
    to savor the journey,
    and to dream of where we'll go next.

Their words remind me:
    not every return is to a place.
Sometimes, it's a reunion with a version of ourselves –
    the part that once loved freely,
        laughed easily,
            and left doors open,
    even if decades passed before stepping back through.

Some journeys end at the threshold, keys in hand.
But the most meaningful returns aren't to places at all –
    they're to each other.

I met Joey & Tricia nearly 40 years ago, vlost touch for 35,
    then picked up where we left off –
    not as strangers, but as a safe place to land.

That's the kind of return worth writing about.

Ode to My Fellow Upgrader ♦
for Metri

You've turned *travel into art* ~
    not just the flights,
    but the way you disappear on Trans-Atlantics
    and **reappear just before landing.**

From our **first around-the-world** trip
    to back-to-back Pacific hops,
    you've been beside me ~
    or slightly ahead,
    boarding early, seat reclined.
    (*thanks to the upgrade* you didn't tell me about).

We've built itineraries ~
    four countries in three days,
    or five layovers for fun,
    just because we could.

You've sweet-talked gate agents,
    outwitted Ops agents,
    and flew on my passes, stealthily.
    I call it legacy.

You built flight loads in XLS,
    learned upgrade and seatmap loopholes,
    boarded flights that shouldn't have happened,
        that "closed gate" is just a suggestion,
    and that charm is a form of clearance.

Because if I taught you to go,
    you taught me **how** to go
        with *style, strategy,*
        and the same grin
    I first saw from across the aisle ~
        your legs dangling,
        feet not yet touching the floor.

Recalculating ♦

Life doesn't always go as planned.
    A storm cancels the ferry.
    A train breaks down mid-journey.
    The itinerary I clung to
        became irrelevant in an instant.

But recalculating
    isn't failure;
    isn't aimless;
    it's resilience disguised as rerouting.

In the *quiet chaos* of change,
    I've learned to breathe deeply,
        to trust the detours,
        to embrace the unplanned as part of the plan.

Like the moment I found myself
    wandering into a *tucked-away alley* in Tokyo,
    guided by nothing but hunger and curiosity ~
    only to discover a ramen shop
    that redefined my understanding of "comfort food."

Or the time my path veered toward a stranger
    in a Parisian park,
    sitting on a bench *sharing a baguette*
    her story intertwining with mine
    for just an afternoon but leaving a lifetime of fulfillment.

The right course isn't always a straight line.

It's the one we find when we stop resisting
    and start recalculating.

Not lost.
Just... rerouted toward something better.

111

The Journeys That Changed Me ♦
A Pilgrimage of Soul, Silence, and Return

Blisters, sore legs, tired limbs
    each step heavy with doubt.
The Way taught me
    to let go of what lay ahead.
Now, on my way home
    after walking The Camino,
    the light poured in.

My soul is different.
Dirty, weary, tired *it held me every mile.*

The desert stripped me bare.
The endlessness taught me
    I am enough.
Now, on my way home
    after aloneness in the Atacama Desert,
    I had been gathered again by silence.

My mind is different.
Still, complete, aware *the hush within me had finally spoken.*

Heavy-hearted and grateful,
    I returned from his quiet bedside.
    His friends, his maps, his photos, his stories.
The man who inspired my steps
    had taken his final journey.
Now, on my way home
    after a last goodbye to my father,
    I held his silence in my chest, and called it a compass.

My love is different.
Sad, inspired, grateful, *grief and gratitude blew over me like wind.*

Alone, sad, numb,
    I was leaving my home
    I was leaving my family.
The sound of life ripping me apart
    was unlike anything I had ever known.
Now, on my way out
    into the world,
    I walked into the world, uncloaked, undone, alive.

My heart is different.
    Born of the journey,
        it is no longer afraid of the fall.
   I still walk,
     changed,

       never standing still.

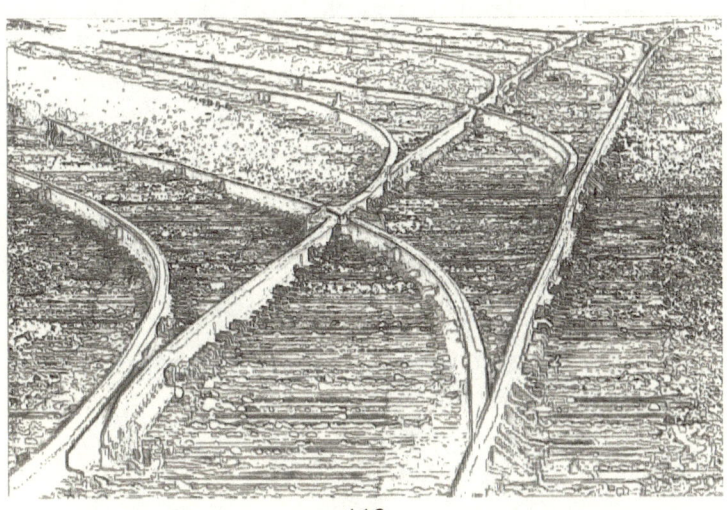

113

Right Train, Wrong Direction ☻

Even professional travelers make **mistakes**.

The kind that leave you staring out a window,
    watching the Mediterranean roll by on the wrong side,
    and realizing - **too late** - that north has become south.

It was Spain. A rush to the airport.
    A train boarded in a hurry, a seat settled into,
    and the assumption that movement meant progress.

But movement is torture
    when you're going the wrong way.

Forty minutes of **helpless** motion.
    No stops.
    No exits.
    Just watching the coast unspool -
        the wrong way,
        while my deadline unspooled with it.

Then, backtracking, a taxi, a sprint through the terminal,
    and somehow, **miraculously**,
    making it just as they were closing the door.

You'd think experience would guard against error,
    but even the best of us can **misread** a moment,
    trust the **wrong instincts**, **board the wrong train**.

Sometimes, the best travel stories
    begin with **the wrong direction.**

Not All Who Wander Stay Gone ♥
Echoes from the Far Side of Familiar

Each journey outward
    whispers the promise of inward steps.
We leave behind the familiar,
    seeking the unknown,
    yet we carry with us
    a hope of finding home anew.

The paths we walk change us,
    not with proclamations,
    but the quiet reshaping of our hearts.

Each step softens the edges,
    polishes the roughness,
    molds us into someone
    who sees the world differently ~
    and who the world sees differently in return.

To return is not to come back as we were,
    but to bring the journey's echoes
    to those who stayed,
    to those we've become.

A memory carried forward, a story shared, a lesson lived.

And sometimes,
    we return not to a place or a person,
    but to the quiet center within ~
    the part of us that wandered far
    just to be found again.

Each return fuels the desire to go;
    each step out begins the longing to return.

We go to return ~
    because not all who wander are meant to stay gone.

I Am Home ♦♥

The place I called home had changed without me.

One day, I paused long enough
        to hear it whisper from within.

I am home.
I am, home.
I, am home.

I am home.

I dreamed of home -
        a place to return,
        my childhood waiting on the horizon.
Its walls would hold my memories,
        its doors would shelter me,
        its light would guide me back.

But the dream was fleeting,
        home, you changed,
        your walls crumbled,
        your horizons shifted.

I called to you across distances:
        "Home, where did you go?
        Why couldn't you wait?
        Why couldn't you stay the same?"

You whispered back through empty rooms,
        through sold houses,
        through childhood streets
            I no longer recognized:

116

I am, home.

But still I searched for you, home,
in postcards sent to old addresses,
in the ache of belonging nowhere,
in the hollow echo of "where are you from?"

"Home," I pleaded with the wind,
"come back to me."

But you had already begun teaching me
the hardest lesson:
you were never in the places
I thought I'd left you.

I, am home.

I realized:
I, am home.
The steady rhythm of my heart,
the sanctuary of my thoughts,
the quiet stillness in the storm.

And further, I learned:
I, am home.
Each breath I take builds my foundation.
Each step I walk lays my path.
Each journey outward returns me inward,
a path that leads me home.

I have been carrying home all along.
And that is enough.

117

A Compass Without a Map

Every path, every street in the world
is your walking meditation.

~ Thich Nhat Hanh

Not every journey begins with certainty.

Sometimes,
 the places that call to us don't arrive with directions.
We stand at the **edge of possibility**,
 knowing only that we must go -
 though we may not yet know why.

Perhaps the greatest decisions aren't made with logic,
 but with *longing*.
Maybe the pull of a place is reason enough.

Have you ever felt the pull of a place before you even arrived?
Do we choose to travel, or does the journey choose us?

What is the difference between longing for
 somewhere new and
 longing for escape?

The decision to go is rarely about logistics - it's about trust.
 Trusting that the road ahead will reveal itself,
 that the unknown is worth stepping into.

A compass without a map still points in a direction.

What happens when the compass spins?

When the pull we feel
    isn't toward a distant shore
    but toward something deeper -
    a journey that can't be booked,
    a destination that has no coordinates?

Sometimes the greatest adventure
    begins not with movement,
    but with stillness.
Not with departure,
    but with arrival -
    arrival at the place
    where we finally stop running.

The compass still points true,
    but now it points inward.

There are journeys that require us
    first to learn how to stand,
    how to breathe,
    how to be present
    in the space we occupy.

Before we can follow the compass
    to distant places,
    we must learn to follow it
    to the foreign country
    that is ourselves.

      The question is not just: Do we dare follow it?
      But: Are we ready for where it leads -
      not just in the world,
      but *within ourselves*?

Different Courage ♥
What Travel Taught Me About Staying Home

While I chased horizons,
    they built foundations.

While I collected passport stamps,
    they collected quiet moments -
    morning coffee rituals,
    neighborhood friendships that deepened,
    gardens that grew season by season.

I returned with stories of distant places.
They had stories too:
    the promotion finally earned,
    the child who learned to read,
    the parent they cared for.

I thought motion was growth.
They knew stillness could be, too.

Both ways of being
    feed the same hunger -
    to matter,
    to discover,
    to become.

I learned their constancy
    was not settling
    but choosing -
    choosing depth over breadth,
    commitment over curiosity,
    presence over possibility.

Different courage.
Same heart.

Their path was not mine.
Mine was not theirs.
Both led somewhere beautiful.

Appendix:

For the Traveler's Return

THE ENDLESS JOURNEY

I once held that stillness was safety.

That grounding meant staying in place, feet firmly planted.
But, healing did not through retreat, but through movement.
Through stepping forward,
    even when I didn't know where the path would lead.

Once, I stood at a different kind of threshold.
Not an airport gate, not a train station,
    but a place where I had to decide
        if my journey was finished.

Travel had been my constant,
    but I first needed to learn how to stand,
    how to breathe,
    how to be.

Step by step, I found my way back to the road.
Not to escape, but to return -
    not to a place, but to myself.

Travel has always been more than motion.
It is a conversation between longing and belonging,
    between the past and the present,
    between the person we are and the one we are becoming.

We leave places behind,
    but they never quite leave us.

A café on a quiet street in Paris,
    the smell of paella rising from a kitchen in Seville,
    the laughter of strangers on a midnight train to nowhere.

We gather these moments like loose pages of a book
    that is always being written but never quite finished.

Perhaps that is why nostalgia holds such power -
not because we wish to relive the past,
but because we recognize the fragments of ourselves
    we left behind in those faraway places.

A journey does not end simply because the ticket is stamped,
the wheels touch home soil, or the bag is unpacked.

Travel lingers.

In the scent of a city still caught in the folds of a scarf.
In the way silence feels heavier
    after the chatter of a foreign café.
In the restless longing stirred by
    a photograph,
    a song,
    a familiar taste in an unfamiliar place.

We return,
    but not as the same traveler who once left.
The version of us that first stepped onto the road
    has been softened, stretched, unraveled, rebuilt.

And so, the journey continues:
    not always in motion, but in memory.
    not in distance, but in depth.
    not in length, but in longing.

The traveler never truly stops moving,
    not because of an insatiable need for new places,
    but because the world itself moves through them.

Some of us will continue wandering, some will have never left.
Others will carry home with them
    and others will seek it forever.

And some will begin to sense something more:
    a whisper beneath the footsteps.
    a presence in the empty streets before dawn.
    a journey unfolding within as the external journey slows.

The Journey Continues

This book is one perspective on the traveler - the journey as
transformation. But there are many ways to move.

Some travelers experience the road through romance - not just
with people, but with places, with fleeting moments, with the
intoxicating rush of possibility.

Others embrace the journey with humor and reluctance,
cursing every flight delay while secretly loving the chaos.

Still others leave parts of themselves behind - unfinished
stories, longing for what was pondering what could have been.

And some begin to walk a different path entirely, the path
    where travel is no longer about the world, but:
        the self,
        the soul, and
        the silent truths whispered between the steps.

Perhaps you've found yourself here.

The Road Ahead

Travel is never finished.

Even as you read these words,
    another journey is already forming:

        perhaps a journey of movement.
        perhaps a journey of meaning.
        perhaps, if you listen closely,
            the path is calling your name.

Wherever it takes you, may it change you.

**May your travels take you far and
    may they always bring you home.**

For in the end, the greatest journey
    is not one of miles,
    but of meaning.

~ Jim

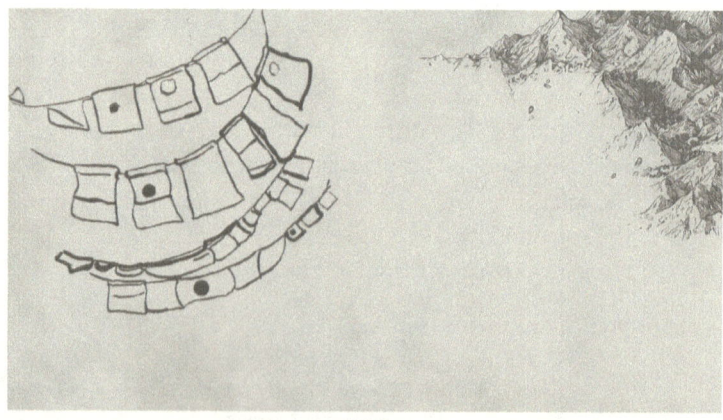

From TV Ads to Travel Apps
By Fred W. Menge

In appreciation of my father, Fred W. Menge,
who penned this poem, Gullible's Travels, in the 1970s...

I can still see him at the kitchen table or on the couch with his
Budweiser, a legal pad balanced on his knee, rhyming words
scribbled along the margins in his all-caps architectural hand-
writing.

He was the one who introduced me to the magic of words and
worlds beyond our small city. Every Saturday, he'd take my
brothers and me to the public library, an old coral-built struc-
ture where the children's section was tucked into a step-down
corner. While we explored, he'd vanish into the stacks and
return with armloads of books and a quiet smile.

Dad was a consummate wordsmith. Each morning, he'd claim
the newspaper first—folding the pages lengthwise the way they
did in New York, where he grew up. His Uncle Joe mailed us
crossword puzzles and Times sections, which Dad filled with
that same perfect hand.

He saw patterns everywhere: in words, rhymes, and the absur-
dity of a world that convinced people to buy what they didn't
need. Gullible's Travels was his gentle satire of 1970s com-
mercials, but also a father's way of teaching his sons to think
critically about the world selling to them.

First published in Southwind Magazine, this poem reminds me
of his patient work at a time when publishing meant typewrit-
ers, envelopes, and long waits.

Thanks, Dad.

I see the world because of you.

GULLIBLE'S TRAVELS

By Fred W. Menge

TV programs are appealing
I don't like to hurt their feelings
Makes me feel that I'm square dealing
When I buy what they are wheeling
If I don't, I feel I'm stealing
so I must buy though I'm reeling
as I've many cures for healing
stacked up high from floor to ceiling.

I have drops for runny nose,
pads galore for calloused toes,
scads of pills when tension shows,
also those when stomach goes.
Several if I fail to doze,
aids for constipation woes,
others when a headache grows
and many more for ulcer's foes.

Hair oils should I chase a dame,
Pep-ups when my hair is lame,
others if I'm really game,
and one makes rivals hide in shame.
Another has a sexy name
and one that gives me grayless fame
there's one that boasts the greatest claim
it even makes a tiger tame.

131

As sporting programs I love dear,
naturally I'm stocked with beer,
so many brands from far and near
that I can't see those in the rear.
Too many now I have a fear,
that should the agents care to peer
down in my cellar, I would hear
the Judge say "Buddy, take a year."

My garage stores pet food now
more different brands than laws allow
enough to make me wipe my brow,
I must get rid of them somehow.
Since cases broke and scattered chow
my neighbors are all in row;
all day long the dogs Bow Wow
and every night, the cats meow

I've soaps of all kinds by the score
piled up back of every door.
There's some for dishes that you pour,
and some for doing laundry chore.
There's those enjoyed in showers roar
and one that was a dove before,
but I don't need those for the floor
'Cause I can't find it any more.

I've beauty aids for lady fair
stacked up nearly everywhere.
Cigarettes in cartons share
with cereals, the cellar stair.
I've shirts and clothes of wash and wear
and toothpastes that give teeth a glare.
I've many brands of coffee rare,
there's not a piece of floor that's bare.

Now no more space, how I regret,
I wonder why, how did I let
those TV ad men make me get
so many things, so deep in debt.
But worst of all, what makes me sweat,
no more can I watch Dave and Chet
as back of all this stuff is yet
hidden now, my TV set.

Originally published in **Southwind Magazine**, circa 1970s

Thanks for the inspiration, Dad.

SCROLLABLE'S TRAVELS
Confessions of an Optimization Addict

Booked on BA with AA miles,
but Air France crew served with smiles.
Three airlines for my boarding files,
codeshare madness spans for miles.

Then tried with points through Bilt and Chase,
clicked too fast, and scored the wrong place.
I called support; they said with grace,
"We'll help you out... just hold your place."

SeatGuru said, "Avoid row ten,"
and ExpertFlyer warned again.
The chart was red, then green, then when ‑
I checked too long ‑ lost seat again.

Amtrak's app showed "on time" lies,
the train was late to no surprise.
Missed connections, travel dies,
three Chicago days ‑ what a prize.

I fed AI my TripIt thread ‑
from Florence trains to Sitka's sled.
It scanned each mishap, crisis, dread,
then said, "Delays are truth," and fled.

My dad filled shelves with soaps and brew,
I've caches stuffed with cookies too.
His stuff was stacked, mine's just askew ‑
but both reveal what scrolls us through.

You warned me once, now I think twice,
Thank you Dad for your advice,
I've mastered deals with great device,
but lost the joy ‑ that was the price.

See you on the other side (of Security), Dad!

ABOUT THE
AUTHOR

Jim Menge is a storyteller, traveler, and seeker of meaning in motion. With a life spent exploring the world's farthest corners, he offers a unique perspective on the intersection of travel, wisdom, and the human experience. His journeys have taken him across continents, through bustling cities and quiet landscapes, always searching for the moments that transform a trip into something deeper - a revelation, a connection, a story worth telling.

A passionate advocate of immersive travel, Jim believes the best journeys are never just about the destination - but about how they change us. His work, infused with humor, insight, and a touch of wanderlust, invites readers to see travel as more than an itinerary. It's an invitation to discover something new - not just in the world, but within ourselves.

As the author of Ode of the Traveler and other works exploring the poetry, philosophy, and sometimes cranky realities of travel, Jim captures both the beauty and absurdity of the journey. Whether it's the joy of unexpected encounters or the frustration of a never-ending security line, his words resonate with anyone who has ever packed a bag and set out in search of something more.

When he's not on the road or deep in conversation about the art of travel, Jim shares his insights as a speaker, consultant, and travel raconteur. His work reflects a lifelong commitment to understanding the world - one step, one story, one ode at a time.

At the ending,

The plane has landed and arrived at the gate ~
it's time to walk the jetbridge.

The ship has reached the port ~
it is time to disembark.

The train has come to the station ~
it's time to offboard.

The car has been parked in the garage ~
it is time to go inside.

I lay down my backpack,
it is time to take off the boots.

The memories I carry,
the happiness,
the wandering,
the time,
the pain,
the loss,
and the moving on
of writing this has not come to end,
but to a place of gratitude to the path.

I set the page aside
a different person
than when I started
and take one last look before I go.

These are not just odes of travel -
they are odes of the traveler:
carried in pockets, scribbled on napkins,
whispered between departures.

JIM MENGE